W9-AHV-045

BACKYARD
LIVING

Outdoor Style

Time-Life Books is a division of Time Life Inc.

TIME LIFE INC.

Chairman and CEO — Jim Nelson
President and COO — Steven L. Janas

TIME-LIFE TRADE PUBLISHING

Vice President and Publisher — Neil Levin
Senior Director of Acquisitions and Editorial Resources — Jennifer Pearce
Director of New Product Development — Carolyn Clark
Director of Marketing — Inger Forland
Director of Trade Sales — Dana Hobson
Director of Custom Publishing — John Lalor
Director of Special Markets — Robert Lombardi
Director of Design — Kate McConnell

OUTDOOR STYLE

Senior Editor — Linda Bellamy
Technical Specialist — Monika Lynde
Production Manager — Carolyn Bounds
Quality Assurance — Jim King, Stacy L. Eddy

Produced by Lark Books, Asheville, North Carolina.

Project Editor — Kathy Sheldon
Art Director — Thom Gaines
Principal Photographers — Evan Bracken
Robin Dreyer
Richard Hasselberg
Photo Stylists — Skip Wade and Thom Gaines
Illustrator — Orrin Lundgren
Watercolorist — Lorraine Plaxico
Proofreader — Carolyn Bertram
Indexer — Catharine Sutherland

Pre-Press Services, Time-Life Imaging Center
Printed in China.
10 9 8 7 6 5 4 3 2 1

TIME-LIFE is a trademark of Time Warner Inc., and affiliated companies.

ISBN 0-7370-0623-4

CIP data available upon application:
Librarian, Time-Life Books
2000 Duke Street
Alexandria, VA 22314

Books produced by Time-Life Trade Publishing are available at a special bulk discount for promotional and premium use. Custom adaptations can also be created to meet your specific marketing goals. Call 1-800-323-5255.

Outdoor Style

AMY ELIZABETH COOK

Contents

Introduction

*O*utdoor Style—what an intimidating concept! Perhaps for you, the phrase conjures up gardens fraught with expensive statuettes and trendy frou-frou. *Style* is something that home-and-garden gurus and their high-gloss magazines hoist over their heads like trophies. What they don't tell you is that *style* is (believe it or not) something that you already have. Of course you do! It's that inimitable touch that you add (however unknowingly) to everything that you do.

This book is designed to help you use that distinctive manner of expression to create a backyard that's yours —not ours. How? Each chapter is chock-full of inspired ideas, explicit how-to instructions, and dazzling color photographs—everything you need to decorate the garden *your* way. Survey the options: Choose from cool hard slate, soft rich moss, and more to build a path or patio that's uniquely yours; find the lighting system, lamps, and fixtures that best brighten your backyard; select a suncatcher made of your favorite patterned glass, and much, much more.

The outdoors is an infinite, never-ending space. With a decorative selection that's just as vast, how does the weekend gardener keep from getting overwhelmed? *Easy.* We've simplified your alfresco space to what's elemental: Water, Light, Air, and Earth. It doesn't get any more basic than that!

You'll start by learning all about water features in the garden, including falls, fountains, and birdbaths— you'll even find step-by-step directions for building your own rustic koi pond! Next, follow our guide to using light in the garden. Plant a striking array of ornamental grasses that filter and reflect the sun, or collect a fanciful assortment of lanterns and luminaries—including one you can make yourself. Now, lift your head to the sky and feel the fresh air wafting through your garden. Celebrate the sky spanning above your outdoor space by positioning ornamental wind toys, both fun and functional, throughout your yard. Finally, use the detailed information in the chapter on earth to give your yard a facelift (whether drastic or subtle) by adding raised beds, berms, terraces, paths, and patios.

So you see, contrary to what you've been told, style is yours already. Use this book to find ways to put it to use—and watch as your garden is transformed into a place of casual refinement, formal elegance, flea-market chic, or whatever describes your outdoor style.

water

Imagine life without water. Impossible, isn't it? Societies have always gathered along coastlines, ports, rivers, and channels. The desire to bring water features to the backyard is a natural one. In this chapter, we'll give you techniques and inspiration to do just that.

First, reflect upon the peaceful delights of still water. Placid pools, even small ones, can mirror so much light that they visually enlarge your outdoor space. Whether you choose to dig a rustic koi pond, install a formal pool, or simply fill a decorative basin, still water will bring serenity to your backyard in a way that nothing else can.

Where still water calms, moving water stimulates. The subtle song of water in motion—be it a trickle, splash, gurgle, or spray—invigorates the spirit and keeps mosquitos away as well. Adding a stream, falls, or fountain to your yard is easier than you might think, and the effect is sure to be dazzling.

Finally, plants and animals need water too! Follow our tips to keep your garden's thirst quenched so blooms stay lush and bright, and learn how water can help attract wildlife to your yard. In no time at all, you'll have turned your backyard into a veritable oasis!

Ponds and Pools

Still water—the jewel of any garden—can be yours with less labor than you might imagine. The satin surface of a pond or pool, no matter its shape or size, glows with quiet color and tranquil light. Here, survey the water gardening options available to you, and discover one that's just right for your backyard.

CONTAINER WATER GARDENS

You wouldn't till a field before you knew that you could grow a seedling in a flowerpot. Similarly, it's a little premature to dig a pond before you're sure that you can care for a smaller ecosystem. A container water garden is a great starting point for the novice water gardener. Whether

you fill a shallow concrete basin (shown to the left) or stock a deep, wide barrel with lilies, containers are the quickest, easiest way to bring water into your outdoor setting.

A shallow dish is the simplest option and despite its small size is sure to affect any landscape. Maintenance is minimal: Simply add the occasional dose of *Bacillus thuringiensis*, available at your local garden supply store. This bacterial insecticide controls mosquito larvae but is harmless to beneficial insects, pets, and humans.

Larger containers may invite the addition of plants. Trays, pots, and barrels all make good portable water gardens. Just be sure that the inner surface is nonporous to prevent leaks. For example, check to see that ceramic pots are glazed or sealed, and line wooden whiskey barrels with PVC before filling.

For easy water gardening, select low-maintenance plants—lilies and lotuses are often safe choices. Several varieties of the *Chromatella* are especially agreeable: 'Attraction' (yellow), 'Aflame' (red), and 'Hal Miller' (white). No matter which you choose, it's important to keep plants away from moving water. Resist the urge to add a fountain, and when refilling, submerge the end of the hose to prevent surface disturbance. Also, site containers in full sun, where plants are sure to flourish. One or two small semitropical fish (such as gambusia) should be able to survive the heat of the water garden and will help control insects.

RAISED POOLS AND OTHER OPTIONS

When you become a more confident water gardener, consider installing a larger water feature. Create an instant centerpiece in your backyard by building a raised pool. The well-defined base of an above ground pool exaggerates its shape and form and provides a great opportunity to integrate decorative masonry into the garden. Raised pools are fairly easy to build, whether you use a pond liner, a preformed pond, or poured concrete.

For a more rustic appeal, opt for an in-ground koi pond. Full instructions for installing such a feature can be found on the pages that follow.

BRIDGES

Just because your backyard lacks a meandering stream is no reason to do without the charm of a simple footbridge. Combining practicality and ornamentation, bridges can be used to span both natural and manmade water features. Perched on the edge of a small pool, a bridge can provide the perfect platform for observing the aquatic life teeming below.

You can purchase a ready-made bridge, but depending on the design and materials you prefer, most small bridges are fairly easy to build. The simplest is a flat plank bridge, which is a primarily functional garden feature. Although arched bridges are slightly more challenging to construct, their quiet grace makes the extra work worth your while. Either style of bridge may visually overwhelm smaller water features—a series of small stepping stones is a more subtle option.

The accessibility and workability of wood make it the most popular bridge material, especially for the do-it-yourselfer. An elegant Japanese-style stone bridge can be stunning in the right setting, but few weekend gardeners have the stonemason's prowess necessary to build such a structure. Stone-faced concrete, while presenting construction challenges of its own, can be a simpler, more viable alternative.

Rustic Backyard Pond

Ponds and pools are timeless sources of sights, scents, and sounds that bring unrivaled tranquility to the garden. A carefully planned pond, brimming with life, can impact your landscape in striking new ways. What's more, installing a pond is much easier than it may sound, especially when you follow these simple directions.

TIPS

- The ideal site for your water feature will be away from trees. An umbrella of leaves will shield aquatic plants from much-needed sunlight. Come autumn, the leaves will scatter on the pond's surface and disturb its delicate ecosystem. Too, you'll want to avoid areas of significant root growth, and low-lying areas where rainwater runoff may disrupt your pond's pH.

- Any garden center that carries water features and accessories should have a staff member who can help you select a pump, filter, and appropriately sized tubing for your pond.

- For safe pump operation, plug it into a moistureproof electrical outlet with a Ground Fault Circuit Interrupter (GFCI).

- Your pond will look much smaller once you've added rocks and plants around the edges. For this reason, choose a preformed pond that is somewhat larger than what you think you'll need.

- Sustain the health and beauty of your pond by stocking it with fish and oxygenating plants. Fish enhance the pond's health—and yours—by dining on mosquitoes and bugs. Remember that pond depth is critical for aquatic plants to thrive; water lilies need 15"- to 36"-deep water.

MATERIALS & TOOLS

- Preformed pond (3' x 4', reinforced plastic or fiberglass)
- Shovel
- Wheelbarrow
- Two straight boards, 3' and 5' long
- Tape measure
- Carpenter's level
- Trowel
- Three 50-pound bags of sand
- Submersible pump (200 to 300 gallons per hour capacity) with filter
- Flexible tubing
- Hose clamp (sized to fit tubing)
- Heavy-duty PVC pipe
- Hacksaw
- Scissors
- PVC liner for waterfall pools
- Assorted stones, rocks, and plants for landscaping edges
- Aquatic plants
- Mulch

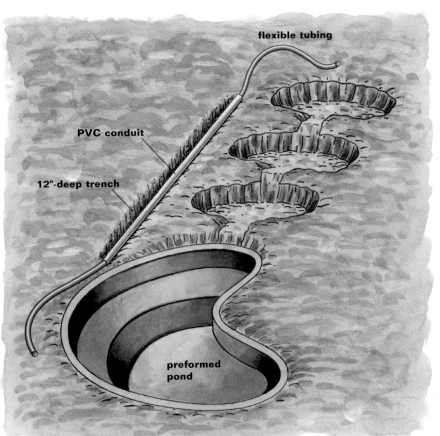

Instructions

1 Place the preformed pond right side up on the selected site. Trace the perimeter of the pond's top rim onto the soil by dribbling handfuls of sand to make an outline. Set the preformed pond aside. (Be sure to trace the outline of the top rim and not the bottom of the pond; the rim will be larger in diameter.)

2 Carefully begin removing soil from within the traced lines, digging 2" deeper and 2" wider than the actual pond form. Pond forms often include ledges, and so they have a smaller diameter at the bottom than at the top. With this in mind, be careful to shape the hole as closely as possible to the contours of the pond form, leaving shelves of soil to support the built-in ledges. Reserve some of the soil that you remove; you'll need it to backfill the hole once the pond form is in place. To check the depth of the hole, place the 5'-long board across the top of the hole. Then use a tape measure to find the distance between the bottom of the hole and the board. (Do not continue with step 3 until the hole is at least 2" deeper than the depth of the pond form. Otherwise, you'll have to repeat some arduous steps later!)

3 Using your shovel and trowel, scrape the bottom of the hole to make it level. Remove large or sharp rocks and any roots or debris. Check whether the bottom of the hole is level by setting the 3'-long board across it and placing the carpenter's level on top of the board. Reposition the board and level several times in order to check for level all the way across the hole's bottom.

7 Install both the submersible pump and the filter, each according to the manufacturer's instructions. Raise the pump above the pond bottom by setting it on bricks; this prevents debris from clogging the intake valve.

8 As is shown in the illustration on page 13, the water in the pond will eventually be pumped up through the flexible tubing to the uppermost waterfall basin. To disguise the tubing, you'll bury it in a 6"- to 12"-deep trench that runs along one side of the three basins and up to the top of the falls. Before digging the waterfall basins, dig the trench for the tubing, setting aside the soil you remove.

4 Spread a 2"-thick layer of damp sand across the bottom of the hole. This will cushion and protect the bottom of the pond form once you've filled it with water. Smooth the sand by running one edge of the 3'-long board across it. Then check the layer of sand by setting the board on it and placing the carpenter's level on top of the board. Repeat to check for level in several different positions.

5 Set the pond form in the hole; its rim should be at ground level. Then check the rim for level by placing the 5'-long board and the carpenter's level across it in various places. To correct the pond form's positioning, remove it from the hole, level the sand again, and replace the shell. Have patience: You may have to repeat this step several times. Removing a water-filled pond to make readjustments later is a task you'll want to avoid!

6 Add 4" of water to the pond form. Next, put some of the sand and reserved soil in your wheelbarrow and mix them. Firmly pack this mixture around the outer wall of the pond form, all the way up to the water level inside. Continue this process, gradually adding water and then backfilling with sand and soil, until the pond is filled with water and is firmly supported around its exterior. As you backfill, make sure there are no gaps under the shelves or around the sides of the pond form.

9 To protect the pump's flexible tubing, encase it in a length of rigid PVC pipe before you bury it. Measure the length of the trench, and then use a hacksaw to cut a piece of PVC pipe to that length. Slip the flexible tubing into the pipe, leaving several feet of exposed tubing at each end. Then place the pipe and tubing in the bottom of the trench and refill the trench. (Alternatively, you may fill the trench with mulch. If the tubing ever needs repairs, you'll find that removing the mulch from the trench is easier than removing heavy soil.)

10 To begin making the waterfalls, scoop out three basins above the pond as shown in the illustration on page 13. Each basin should be approximately 2' to 3' in diameter (the depths may vary) and 3" to 1" higher than the one beneath it. Be careful to slant the floor of each basin slightly backward so that the water pools before overflowing. At the front of each basin, shape a 4"- to 6"-long sill (the canal through which water flows as it drops to the basin below).

11 Measure and cut a separate sheet of PVC liner for each basin, allowing enough space for all of the following: the diameter and depth of the basin and sill; a generous overlap from basin to basin; and plenty of extra liner (at least 6" in all directions) to overlap the soil surrounding the basin. Starting with the bottom basin, line each basin and sill, pressing the liner into each hole firmly. Then trim the excess liner, leaving at least 6" to overlap the edges of each basin. Cover these edges with soil.

12 Arrange the loose upper end of the tubing in the uppermost basin; attach the lower end to the pump and secure with a hose clamp. Then arrange stones, rocks, and plants around the pond and basin sites. Use only smooth stones on any exposed portions of the liner, since sharp stones might tear the plastic.

13 Turn the pump on and continue to add water to the pond until both the pond and basins are full. Now comes the fun part: Creating the series of small waterfalls! Position smooth stones and rocks in the basins and on their sills. Experiment as much as you like, arranging stones and rocks to create varied ripples and rapids. Rearranging stones at the edge of each fall will produce changes in both the sound of the water and its appearance.

14 Add soil around and between the rocks at the edges of the pond and basins, and put in some plants. You won't want to plant anything directly over the buried PVC conduit and tubing, as you may need

to uncover them in the event of repair. To disguise the trench line, arrange rocks over the top, or just cover it with an attractive mulch.

15 Now you're ready to think about stocking your pond with aquatic plants and fish. In order to determine how many creatures your pond can host, consider not the number of fish but rather the "inches of fish." For each square foot of the surface of your pond, you may add ⅔' to ¾' of fish. Be sure to wait a week or two to allow the ecosystem to stabilize before bringing fish to their new home.

Birdbaths

A backyard birdbath is proof positive that a water feature in the garden is more than just visually pleasing; it's functional as well. Water is as vital as food to the life of an animal. Winged creatures enjoy both the sustenance and recreation that a birdbath offers, and you'll enjoy the fascinating show they put on. With the utmost of grace, a bird dips the ends of its wings in the water, then touches its oily preening gland with its bill. Feather by feather, the bird grooms itself, drawing each bit of its coat through its bill. The exception is the robin, which splashes about unabashedly until it's literally too waterlogged to fly away.

BIRDBATH BASICS

Choosing the right site for your birdbath may be literally a matter of life and death—for the birds, anyway. Keeping the birdbath out of the path of predators is essential. While pedestal baths are safe tucked into high grasses or shrubbery, nestling a ground-level bath into foliage is a dinner invitation to a hungry cat, and birds will avoid it for fear of attack. Keep ground-level baths out in the open, at least several feet away from flower borders.

Light but regular maintenance of your birdbath will keep feathered friends healthy. Replenish the water weekly, and scrub out the dish with a

stiff brush and water several times each season. As winter approaches, water may become icy, but thirsty birds will try to drink anyway. Harsh chemicals—often touted as antifreezing agents—spell disaster for a bird's fragile digestive system. Instead, cover the dish with plastic-coated wire mesh, or place twigs in a grid above the water. This keeps birds' delicate feet out of the ice-cold water while still allowing them to lean down for a drink. The more dedicated birder may want to regulate water temperature with a special heater, available at most home and garden stores.

DECORATIVE BIRDBATHS

Along with luring wildlife to your backyard, a birdbath also gives you the chance to add a personal touch to your garden. Place a colorfully-painted saucer or odd china dish beneath a dripping outdoor faucet to create an impromptu birdbath. Or, do without the saucer and just scatter polished glass or marbles across the dampening earth. Swallows and robins will perch on the gleaming bits to collect mud pellets for their nests. The moisture will also keep earthworms within beak's reach for robins—a rarity in drought season.

Another option is to purchase a commercial birdbath. Your local garden supply center should sell a variety of styles, from hanging saucers to pedestal-mounted baths. Note that many pedestal baths feature a removable dish, which eases the task of cleaning the birdbath. Fanciful designs, such as the one shown at left, abound, or you may transform an unadorned birdbath by slathering it with grout and affixing ceramic shards, as shown below.

Want to host more bathers than a small dish will accommodate? Try

digging a shallow pool. (This venture is much less ambitious than constructing an actual pond as shown on page 12.) First, define the shape of your pool by carving into the sod with the tip of a shovel. Then, lift out the dirt to reveal a shallow (3- to 5-inch-deep) depression. Prevent mud puddle syndrome by fashioning a simple liner for your ornithological oasis. Simply smear a sheet of plastic with non-toxic adhesive; then sprinkle it with sand and let it dry. This textured liner will give tiny bird feet more traction than ordinary plastic. Conceal unsightly edges by weighing them down with decorative stones. Place another pile of stones in the center so that small birds can play safely; then fill the pool with water.

Water for Rest and Relaxation

Why should the koi have all the fun? From the sacred waters of the Ganges to the colorful commercial water parks of modern times, we humans experience a certain sense of joy and peace in the presence of water. Ancient societies worshiped wells and springs, and today we still seek water for spiritual, medicinal, and recreational purposes. Whether it's a sprint through the garden sprinkler or a few laps in the backyard pool, experience the invigorating effects of water in your own backyard.

SPAS AND SWIMMING POOLS

It sometimes seems the hardest part of installing a spa or pool is justifying it. Even with their history of meeting health and medicinal needs, both features maintain reputations as mere luxuries. This reputation is ill-deserved: The word spa, after all, was originally an acronym for a Roman emperor's declaration, *"sanitas per aquas,"* meaning "health through water." A warm dip in a hot tub, for example, allows insomniacs to slumber more sweetly, arthritics to move with greater ease, and workaholics to slow their breakneck pace.

Adding a swimming pool is, of course, a major undertaking—and an expensive one at that. But few features offer more in the way of recreation and relaxation. Your whole family can enjoy the health advantages of a pool. Swimming is a form of exercise that challenges and strengthens the entire body. Even if you're not an eager swimmer, you'll enjoy splashing around in the cool blue depths.

Spas and pools also serve a decorative function in the backyard. Sparkling water can highlight colorful tilework lining the water feature or can set off carefully laid decking or nearby landscaping. Surround a hot tub with a planted trellis, or light up your swimming pool with a sea of floating candles for your next soiree. During the daylight hours, the light that the water reflects will send glints and glimmers all over your yard.

MAINTENANCE AND SAFETY

Like any body of water, spas and swimming pools also present a certain danger. Observing some basic safety precautions will ultimately make for a more gratifying experience. An enclosed fence will keep out wandering children or pets and is actually required by law in many areas. Lifesaving gear, rope and float lines, a pool cover, and adequate lighting are other accessories that may prepare you for what might otherwise be an emergency. Your spa or hot tub manufacturer should provide you with other important safety considerations, none of which need spoil your fun.

Keeping your pool, spa, or hot tub in top operating condition is vital not only to the safety of those who use the facilities, but to the safekeeping of what can be a sizeable financial investment. Familiarize yourself with your pool and

spa equipment, and give it a careful visual inspection regularly. Anything that looks broken, worn, or frayed warrants professional consultation and repair. Clean and chemically balance the water often—no one wants to dive into murky waters, and improper pH can corrode pool equipment.

OTHER OPTIONS

Even if a spa or swimming pool is a bit extravagant for your tastes (or your budget), a backyard oasis remains within your grasp. For example, on page 20, we've shown you an easy, inexpensive installation for an outdoor shower. Indulge in an herbal footbath on your patio, or frolic with your children in the cool spray of a sprinkler. Even those with limited free time and budgets can experience water's revitalizing qualities.

Outdoor Showers

I s the prospect of installing a pool or hot tub too daunting but the thought of joining your kids in their plastic wading pool just plain depressing? Then dog-ear this page of the book: You're the perfect candidate for an outdoor shower. The materials are inexpensive, the labor is nominal, and the resulting luxury is indescribable! Here, you'll find a review of the most basic elements of an outdoor shower and a walk-through of the installation process. If, after a thorough read, you still find the project to be beyond your D.I.Y. capabilities, then consult a plumber or a detailed guide.

WHERE TO BEGIN

Before you even buy the hardware, you'll need to choose a location for your shower. (Don't let your imagination get the best of you, though; your home's preexisting pipe work will largely dictate the site. This means that placing a freestanding oasis in the far corner of your rose garden may be a little ambitious!) Start with a trip to your basement. Check the layout of your plumbing to find a logical place to extend both hot and cold pipelines to the outdoors. Because each house is equipped with a different water delivery system, the required extensions, called branches, will follow their own unique paths.

Locate the spot on the basement wall where the hot and cold pipes will travel outward; then carefully burrow two parallel holes, using a method appropriate to the building materials of your house. Now, turn your home's main water valve (usually located on the inlet side of the water meter) to the "off" position. You're ready to start the pipe work.

SHOWER COMPONENTS

Variations on the outdoor shower abound, but the simplest version is illustrated to the right. The fixtures can be made of copper, galvanized metal, or PVC; talk to a consultant at your local home improvement center about the material that will best suit your purposes. Once you've extended the hot and cold water pipes (A) through the exterior wall of your house, add a T-connector (B) to the end of each. These pieces will channel water both up to the shower head and down to the center spigot (C). Using a combination of risers (D), quarter-turn ball valves (E), and elbows (F), piece together a rectangular assembly like the one shown.

WHAT NEXT?

Before you reward your fledgling plumbing efforts with a long, cool shower, be sure to make provisions for adequate drainage. This is no after-thought: A well-drained site not only

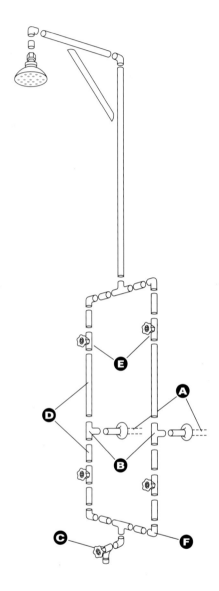

protects the foundation from rot and the basement from floods, it also prevents erosion of the surrounding landscape.

Prepare the site in much the same way as you would for a path (page 90) or a patio (page 98), using pin flags to stake out a base measuring four feet square. Because the site will be con-

stantly drenched with water—unlike a path or patio—you'll need to dig especially deep. Excavate no less than one foot of soil. Fill the pit with gravel, and top it off however you like (see "Paving Possibilities" on page 92). Consider laying tile for a Mediter-ranean theme, or etch concrete with decorative textures and patterns. For simplicity's sake, you might instead lay a wooden doormat to protect feet from sharp gravel, or just set a large, flat stone in place.

CREATING PRIVACY

If your shower is already hidden from the view of your neighbors, you may not care to erect a wall around the site. If, however, your neighborhood resem-bles most of suburbia with yards squeezed tightly together, then create a nook for your outdoor shower. The walls will contribute a great deal to the atmosphere of the shower, so examine your options. Raise a trellis and let it thicken with viney growth, or construct a simple wooden fence and give it a bright, cheery paint job. Or try bolting together an aluminum frame and lash on striped canvas. No matter what type of enclosure you come up with, leave the ceiling open! You'll enjoy nothing more than a refreshing blast of water under a brilliant cobalt sky.

Water for Plants

Plants, the main decorative feature of your backyard, cannot survive without water. A haphazard approach to watering will damage your plants, your bank account, and precious natural resources. Establish a system to get the water where it's needed when it's needed, and you'll save time and money as well as your drooping delphiniums.

There are two primary approaches to watering your garden: sprinkling and soaking. Sprinkling works well for lawns, seedlings, ground covers, and plants that thrive in high-humidity environments. It rinses dust and pollutants from foliage and discourages insects. Soaking (which sends water directly to the plants' root zones) is best for roses, bulbs, and other plants prone to fungal diseases. Systems that use the drip or soaking method of irrigation can save up to 70 percent of the water used by sprinkler systems. They are essential in very dry, hot conditions where water evaporates quickly. Gardeners in drought-prone areas and arid climates will want to find an appropriate soaking system. Additionally, gardeners with narrow beds in any clime may find that soaking saves water that sprinklers waste. Consider the following methods of sprinkling and soaking your way to a backyard oasis.

RAINWATER

One quarter of an inch of rain on a 1000-square-foot roof yields 150 gallons of water. Don't just sit there listening to the pitter-patter—get yourself a rain barrel! Directing rain gutters into a wine cask, pickle barrel, or big plastic bucket provides you with an easy, free water source. Just fill your watering

Crocosmia

can by dipping it into the container, or insert a hose outlet at the bottom of the container.

SPRINKLERS

The simplest type of sprinkler is a watering can—a favorite of those with container plants and small gardens. More sophisticated sprinklers attach to hoses and come in a range of designs, from impulse to oscillating to stationary systems. Antique, novelty, and handwrought sprinklers (such as the copper one in the photo upper right) can also double as garden ornaments. Choose the type appropriate to your irrigation needs; your local garden center can provide good advice here. Because sprinklers wet stems and foliage, avoid using them on plants prone to fungal disease or in the evening.

Be mindful when positioning your sprinkler that renegade droplets may take to the wind and drench sidewalks rather than soil. Placed away from paved surfaces, though, a sprinkler is an excellent way to keep plants thriving. To maximize water conservation, attach an automatic timer to regulate water flow and set it to operate in the morning when less evaporation will occur.

SOAKER HOSES

Soaker hoses are basically "leaky" hoses—lengths of foam, vinyl, or rubber riddled with holes. To use this extremely efficient type of hose, weave it through your garden so that water will be released over plants' root zones. Then turn on the water at the tap and adjust the pressure to dampen a two- to three-foot-wide band of earth.

DRIP IRRIGATION SYSTEMS

A drip irrigation system is much like an upscale soaker hose, but instead of releasing water along its entire length,

individual components direct hoses to specific areas. By coordinating the drip points with the root zones of individual plants, the system releases water just where it's needed. The drip method allows plants to prosper with less water, and its focus on providing

water to roots instead of foliage helps prevent fungal diseases. System costs are extremely reasonable, especially given the cut your water bill will take once it's installed.

JAPANESE RAIN CHAIN

There's nothing decorative about the standard downspout. While drainage is important to garden maintenance—water flowing from your rooftop erodes soil and destroys plantings—visually appealing alternatives do exist. The most notable is the ancient Japanese rain chain, called *kusari doi* in its homeland.

The concept is simple. A chain runs from the corner eave of the roof straight to the ground. As drops collect in the gutters, they stream towards the chain, which provides a downward watercourse. At the base of the chain, a pool of stones absorbs excess runoff. (Or, direct the rain chain into a barrel, and use the water you've saved on thirsty plants.) You can find traditional chains, intricately wrought of copper, in garden gift stores. If they seem pricey, know that any series of links will suffice. You can even fashion a rain chain of colorful parakeet perches from the pet supply store. The easiest option is probably a simple chain from the hardware store, enhanced if you wish with an oil-based enamel.

Falls and Fountains

Spend a few moments watching and listening to moving water, and you'll find that its revitalizing powers are amazing. The melodious sounds of water in motion have soothed the human soul since 4000 B.C., when the first water gardens appeared in the Middle East. Cascading fountains were common features in Roman courtyards and medieval gardens, and Renaissance gardens were marked by theatrical waterworks. During the seventeenth century, in the grand garden of Versailles, more than one thousand fountains greeted the guests of Louis XIV. Your bank account may not support such opulence, but that's no reason not to enjoy the simple songs of surging falls and fountains.

SMALL FOUNTAINS

Easy assembly, portability, and convenience all account for the ever-growing trend of tabletop and patio fountains. If you're limited by space, budget, or time (or maybe all three)—not to worry: There's a fountain design for anyone who enjoys the magical effects of moving water.

The advent of small submersible pumps allows the weekend gardener to turn almost anything into a fountain. Begin with a creative spirit and a few basic materials from your local garden center; within an hour or two, your fountain will be up and running. You'll need a decorative container to serve as a reservoir from which water is pumped, an appropriately-sized submersible pump, rubber tubing, and materials such as stones, marbles, or plants to cover the hardware. You'll be surprised by the versatility of tabletop fountains. If you tire of a particular container, simply replace it with another that suits your mood. Or modify an existing fountain by choosing a new assortment of surrounding plants and decorative materials.

Fountain themes abound, including a millstone set on a bed of pebbles, a stone basin and antique statuary, or smooth silky water spilling over hand-carved granite onto obsidian stones. For a playful touch, add a gushing gargoyle or a spouting fish. Such adornments are available in most garden centers and catalogs. Many are made from concrete or reconstituted stone, but other choices include bronze, terra-cotta, and fiberglass. Before buying, be sure to find out what kind of pump is required to achieve the desired result.

It's best to locate a small fountain close to an existing electrical outlet (the pump operates on normal household current). You'll also want to place the water feature near your favorite garden seating, so that you can experience its stimulating effects every time you rest in your outdoor space. In a sunny spot, the water will gleam brightly, while a shady location will impart a subtler effect.

Small fountains sit well on a porch or patio during warm weather and are mobile enough to move inside during the colder months. Inside your home, they make handsome displays that promise to inspire your senses on even the dreariest winter days.

FOUNTAINS FOR PONDS AND POOLS

If you already have a pond or pool in your backyard, a fountain can add a dramatic focal point to your landscape design, while the steady sound of rhythmic splashes, sprays, gushes, or gentle gurgles will enhance your experience of relaxing outdoors. When adding a fountain to a water garden, you'll have to consider the effects of moving water on plants and fish. Many aquatic plants, such as water lilies, won't survive the stress of strong underwater currents or the battering of constant splashing. On the other hand, aerated water that's pumped and filtered enhances the health of fish.

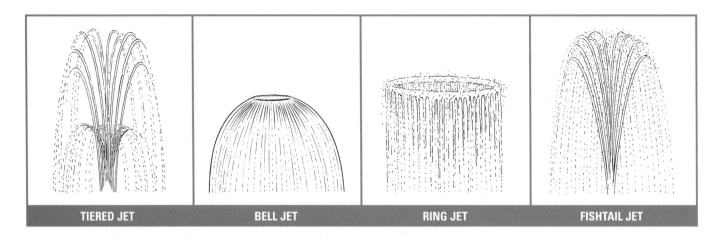

TIERED JET   **BELL JET**   **RING JET**   **FISHTAIL JET**

Creating a balance that allows both plants and fish to thrive is a challenging but critical task.

If your fountain isn't located near an existing outdoor outlet, have an electrician run an underground wire to the site and install an outlet there. Hide wires and cables leading from the outlet to the pump in a length of PVC pipe covered with soil and stones. Be sure to use Ground Fault Circuit Interrupter (GFCI) circuitry and avoid using extension cords.

SELECTING A JET

The glimmering spray of a fountain creates a kind of aquatic sculpture, the form of which is determined by the type of fountain jet you choose. Jets come in a wide range of shapes and patterns, including bubble jets, geysers, multi-tiered jets, tulip jets, and water-bell jets. Some have interchangeable heads that allow you to vary the spray pattern. If you have aquatic plants, then geysers and bell jets are good choices, since they create minimal

pump must be housed in a separate chamber aboveground, usually to the side of the pond. A reinforced inlet hose feeds water from the pond to the pump, which then sends water through a return pipe to the fountain.

In most cases, a submersible pump will meet your needs. Consider a surface pump only if you plan to install a very large water feature with a spray higher than seven feet. Submersible pumps can be found at your local garden center, in sizes and prices to match whatever fountain design you choose. (You may decide to consult an expert for advice on buying and installing a surface pump.) The pumps are self contained, easy to install, require no priming, and often come in a handy kit complete with a T-piece, flow adjuster, and jet.

water disturbance. The simplest jets connect to a cone-shaped outlet or to a T-piece that comes with most small and medium-sized pumps. When choosing a jet, you'll need to consider the size of the fountain and the height of its spray in relation to the dimensions of your pond. You don't want excess water from an oversized fountain splashing onto a patio full of guests! As a general rule, the spray should be no taller than half the pond's width or diameter.

SELECTING A PUMP

Selecting a pump for your fountain can seem more daunting than it actually is. To find a pump that suits the fountain you have in mind, take into account how many gallons per hour it will need to pump to create the spray that you desire. Also, factor in the distance that the water will be pumped. For ponds and pools, the pump should circulate half the volume of the body of water every hour.

There are two basic types of water pumps—submersible and surface (externally mounted). Submersible pumps sit in a pond or pool and force water through a jet or along a piece of tubing to a fountain elsewhere in the pond. For simple installations, the jet is fitted directly on top of the pump by a T-piece with a flow adjuster and an outlet for a waterfall. A surface

Burbling Garden Fountain

Yes—achieving romance in your garden is as easy as we've promised! This simple project will whisk you away from your suburban backyard and into the serene depths of a tropical rainforest. Be sure to read the instructions thoroughly and have all of the supplies readily on hand before you begin.

MATERIALS & TOOLS

- Submersible pump (A)
- Plastic tubing, 1' in length (B)
- Plastic bucket (C)
- Ceramic planter, slightly taller than bucket (D)
- Plastic saucer (E)
- Small decorative bowl (F)
- Ceramic garden ornament (G)
- Collection of polished rocks (H)
- Utility knife
- Awl or ice pick
- Electric drill and masonry bit
- Protective eyewear

TIPS

- The diameter of the plastic tubing should be sized to fit your pump. Meanwhile, the drill bit that you use should create holes that fit snugly around the tubing.
- Use a thin plastic saucer designed to catch drainage from potted plants. Make sure that its diameter is roughly the same as that of the planter that you choose, or cut a larger one to size using your utility knife.
- Ceramic garden ornaments, also called garden "stones," are available at garden specialty stores and pottery outlets. If you have trouble finding one, any waterproof orb that can handle a drill bit will do—holiday ornaments included!
- Before you begin, get acquainted with your pump. Experiment with the water flow by using different lengths of tubing with a variety of pressure settings.

Instructions

1 To begin assembling the base of the fountain (this part is concealed in the finished fountain, but shown in the illustration), turn the submersible pump to the desired setting and fit the plastic tubing over the output valve.

2 Use the utility knife to cut an opening in the top half of the plastic bucket about 2" in diameter (or large enough to accommodate the electrical plug).

3 Set the submersible pump in the bottom of the plastic bucket, snake the electrical cord through the hole you've just created, and place the assembly inside the ceramic planter. Bring the cord to rest over the edge of the planter.

4 Fill the bucket with 4 cups of water, or enough to cover the pump's intake valve by 1". The base of the fountain is complete.

5 With the utility knife, carve a niche in the edge of the plastic saucer sized to fit around the electrical cord. Now, cut a hole in the center of the saucer sized to allow the bowl to rest halfway inside. With the awl or ice pick, pierce a series of holes along the inner rim of the saucer.

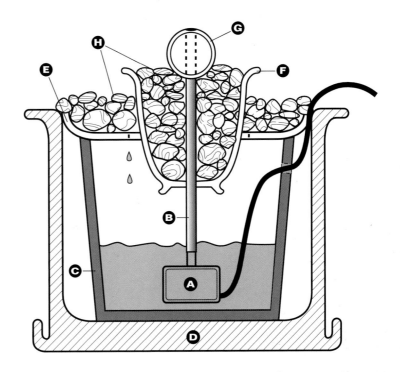

6 Don your protective goggles, and use the drill to bore a hole in the center of the bowl's bottom. While you have the drill handy, make two holes along the axis of the garden ornament, one at the top and one at the bottom.

7 Fit the saucer into the planter so that it rests on top of the plastic bucket. Find the loose end of the plastic tubing, and bring it through the opening in the plastic saucer.

8 Push the tubing through the hole in the bowl, and nestle the bowl into the opening in the saucer.

9 Now, thread the tubing through the garden ornament, gently pulling out the slack. Trim the tubing so that approximately ¼" remains poking out of the ornament.

10 Spread the polished rocks in the tiers created by the bowl and the plastic saucer, taking care to camouflage ragged plastic or other eyesores. Plug in the fountain and observe the flow that it creates. Adjust pump pressure as needed.

GARDEN ART AND WHIMSY

Upper Left: The spiral is an ancient design symbolizing the origin of life. Much like the stone-and-moss arrangement on page 125, this slate-lined pond shows the unique decorative appeal of natural objects.

Tastefully-chosen garden statuary can bring an air of refinement to your backyard. **Above:** A water nymph enjoys an evening dip in the botanical gardens of West Stockbridge, Massachusetts.

Left: An outdoor shower is common enough, but how about a backyard bathtub? With a little ingenuity and some carefully-laid decking, this Canadian homeowner shows us a creative renovation of an antique clawfoot tub—and a rare backyard luxury.

Right: One man's industrial trash is another man's backyard treasure. This surprisingly elegant scrap metal fountain, innovated by Asheville, NC, artist Christopher Mello, graces the Japanese gardens of a mountain spa.

Investing in a fountain ornament is a surefire way to add zest to a backyard water element. **Above:** This whimsical fish leaps high above the massive container water garden that he calls home. **Right:** A lion roars out an aquatic greeting.

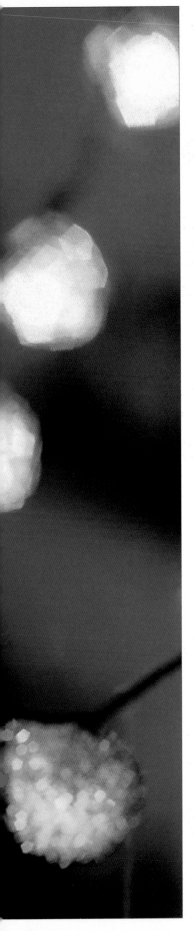

light

Light—a primary source of growth, sustenance, and warmth—needs no introduction. The drama of a single shaft of sunlight filtering through overhead branches, the comfort of a radiant fire, and the grandeur of a strategically lit sculpture all add to outdoor ambience.

Sunlight creates a range of effects throughout the day—a cool haze at dawn, a brazen light at noon, a subtle warmth at dusk. Here, survey suncatching plants that lend beauty to your backyard anytime of day; learn to use greenhouses to channel the sun's energy for growth; and discover how glass and other lustrous materials scatter sunbeams throughout the garden.

Once the sun sets, you'll need a good lighting design to keep your garden aglow. Fire is the classic choice for after-hours illumination; from a single flame to a crackling blaze, our guide will show you how to safely enjoy fire in the outdoors. A less romantic but very practical way to brighten the backyard is to get wired: Nothing beats electric lighting for convenience and utility. Find all of the information you'll need to devise your own backyard lighting scheme—right in these very pages!

Sunlight for Plants

A visionary landscape architect once named the rays of the sun among the gardener's essential raw materials. Right he was: Both the practical and aesthetic success of your garden space depend largely on natural light. Step into your backyard on a summer's day. Observe the greens: the neon chartreuse, the soothing celadon, the deep hunter. All owe their vibrancy to active chlorophyll, which channels the sun's energy for food—and provides a feast for your eyes at the same time.

THE AESTHETICS OF SUNLIGHT

Even the tiniest patch of land, patio, or rooftop can feel boundless when you use the sun as a design element and invite a bit of light into the space. These days, garden shops sell such an array of trinkets and baubles that it's easy to forget that some of the best suncatchers are actually plants.

Clearly the sun is responsible for loud oranges, smooth bright yellows, and soft violets in our flower beds. But what about those underrated foliage plants and grasses? Year-round suncatchers include ornamental grasses, perennials, trees, and shrubs.

In the springtime, for example, the mountain silverbell's delicate parts are set aglow by sun or moonlight. Autumn sun highlights the shrub's foliage, particularly in the morning. Come winter, bright sunlight gives the plant's winged fruits an exaggerated skeletal appearance. At right, you'll find more plants for your garden that will filter the light in unexpected ways.

NATURAL SUNCATCHERS

Plants whose stalks or seed heads are particularly translucent or reflective will cast sunlight around your garden in unique ways. Meanwhile, colored flowers and foliage add vibrancy to your yard. Here are a few especially exquisite all-natural suncatchers.

SPIDER FLOWER
Cleome hassleriana

Lanky spires of green fuzz give way to the fine-petaled pink crowns of the 'Rose Queen' variety of *Cleome*. These self-seeding annuals will quickly fill a herbaceous border, often rising as high as five feet.

ZEBRA GRASS
Miscanthus sinensis 'Zebrinus'

Zebra grass, with its broadly arching green blades, is so named for its variegated patterns of contrasting pale bands, which create an optical illusion with sun-dappled effects.

PAMPAS GRASS
Cortaderia selloana

The tall blades of this plant pale in the autumn to reflect light during the day and create a dramatic silhouette at sunset. The truly striking feature of pampas grass, though, is its long feathering plumes.

COLORADO BLUE SPRUCE
Picea pungens 'Glauca'

The metallic color of this tree gives its foliage an unexpected sheen. When its upright, silvery branches reach out and catch the light (of the sun *or* moon), they deliver year-round radiance to your landscape.

BLACK FLOWERING FOUNTAIN GRASS
Pennisetum alopecuroides 'Moudry'

Fine tufts top the glossy green blades of this plant. While this grass is not quite as tall as other ornamental grasses, it makes a strong visual impact in any backyard.

EUROPEAN WHITE BIRCH
Betula pendula

You'll wish for winter to hurry and whisk the leaves from this tree, revealing a better view of its beautifully stark white bark. This particular birch quickly towers to a stately pyramidal form more than 35 feet tall and 15 feet wide.

Cold Frames, Cloches, and Greenhouses

COLD FRAMES

A cold frame is a wooden or metal box with a cover (known as a light) made from a transparent material such as glazed glass or clear plastic sheeting. Cold frames may either sit directly on the soil, right in a garden bed, or be placed on a deck or patio and used to protect container plants. These simple, covered box structures allow you to extend the growing season and prolong summer harvests by protecting plants well into the winter. They're also used to start seedlings in the early spring.

Maintaining growth in cold frames is simple. Keep a thermometer inside the frame to monitor the interior temperatures, which should be kept at about 70°F (21°C) in the spring and 65°F (18°C) in the fall. Closing the light will raise the temperature by trapping warmth created by the sun. To lower the internal temperature, just open the light and prop it up. (Some cold frames come with built-in temperature gauges that raise and lower the lights automatically.)

In most instances, cold frames need no ventilating during the coldest months of the year, and because the groundwater table is higher during these months, the plants within the frame will probably need no watering. During very early spring and late fall, only the occasional check-in is necessary. The transition months, during

While extremely cold or hot weather can damage plants, sudden changes in temperature are actually much more dangerous to them. In many areas of the continental United States, particularly in mountain and desert climates, extreme temperature swings can destroy a plant's chances of survival. Temperature, wind, and moisture changes are all factors that affect a plant's stability, but there are protective measures you can take to guard your garden and container plants from them. The most effective step you can take is to create a microclimate for your plants—one that will stabilize the temperature, prevent excess moisture from freezing on stems and leaves, and shield delicate plants from harsh winds. Cloches, cold frames, and greenhouses are all used for this purpose.

shops, traditional cloches have no competition when it comes to beauty; their smooth, domed surfaces catch sunlight from all angles.

GREENHOUSES

Greenhouses are best for year-round container gardening and for starting garden plants from seed.

Don't be overwhelmed by the thought of the huge commercial greenhouses that you see being used at nurseries; these just aren't necessary or economical for backyard gardens. Many smaller models are available, however, from shed-sized kits that can be assembled over a weekend and inexpensive plastic "tunnels" that arch over rows of plants to very small, portable conservatories that fit over individual container plants. Let the size of your garden—and budget—guide you as you select an appropriate plant-protection system.

To protect large planted areas in the garden, tunnels work best. They're assembled right where they're needed, by bending fiberglass rods into arches over the soil and covering them with plastic sheeting. Portable, one-plant conservatories, which consist of platforms with glass covers, are similar to cloches and come in all shapes and sizes. They're most often used to protect delicate potted plants and seedlings.

the spring and early fall, when temperatures can fluctuate dramatically, are the ones during which you should keep a close watch on plants. Raise and lower the lights as necessary to keep temperatures stable, and water when you water the rest of the garden. In the summertime, open the lights completely.

CLOCHES

For protecting individual container plants from frost, traditional glass cloches are wonderful garden devices. These small, bell-shaped covers ("cloche" is the French word for bell) are made to be placed right over the plant and container whenever frost is predicted. Unlike traditional cloches, contemporary versions are made with materials ranging from plastic and fiberglass to paper. These provide the same basic services and are sometimes easier to find. Available from gardening centers and antique

Decorative Garden Sundial

TIPS

- The hour markers of this horizontal dial rest on a flat gravel portion known as the **dial plate,** which can be as large or as small as you like. The diameter of the dial shown on the opposite page is approximately six feet.

- The **gnomon** (or shadow-casting part) of this sundial is a slab of scrap marble. You may use any waterproof material you like, as long as it forms a triangle with one 90° angle and one 45° angle.

Instructions

1 Position the curved edging sections to form a circle, adjusting each section as necessary.

2 To mark the area for digging, trickle a line of white flour around the outside of the circle formed by the edging sections.

3 Remove the edging sections and set them aside.

4 Using a shovel, strip the sod from within the marked circle and dig out the soil to a depth of 2" or 3". (Make sure that you don't remove too much soil, or the edging sections will be so low they'll be obscured by the lawn surrounding them.) Scrape the soil at the bottom to make it level.

A lovely addition to any area of your yard that receives full sun, this easy-to-make sundial will keep you in touch with the time whenever you're within sight of it. Do keep in mind, however, that making a truly accurate sundial is a relatively complex undertaking, involving calculations too time-consuming for most backyard hobbyists. Use this simplified version to remind you when to start cooking dinner, but don't try to time your roast beef or baked potatoes with it!

MATERIALS & TOOLS

- **10 curved sections of scalloped brick edging**
- **Several cups of white flour**
- **Shovel**
- **Trowel**
- **Landscape fabric**
- **Scissors**
- **18 bags (½ cubic foot each) of pea gravel**
- **Garden rake**
- **Compass**
- **One triangular slab of granite, with one 90° angle and two 45° angles**
- **12 granite scraps or stones**

5 Cut a circle of landscape fabric to fit inside the circle, and position it on top of the soil. This will help prevent weeds from growing up through the gravel yet allow rainwater to drain away properly.

6 Position the edging sections around the interior perimeter of the circular hole, scraping more soil from the hole if required. Make sure the sections are upright and are supported by the outer edges of the hole; backfill with soil if necessary.

7 Fill the hole with pea gravel and spread it evenly with a garden rake. Be careful not to add too much gravel, or it will spill into your grass. Scoop out some gravel in the center to make space for the gnomon.

8 For real timekeeping accuracy, a gnomon in the Northern Hemisphere should be parallel to the earth's axis or point at the Pole Star. (If you live in the Southern Hemisphere, your gnomon should point to the southern celestial pole.) This decorative sundial, however, makes no pretenses to complete accuracy; its gnomon will face magnetic north. Stand inside the gravel dial plate, and use your compass to locate magnetic north; then carefully position the gnomon so that its vertical edge is facing in that direction.

9 Level the gravel around the gnomon. (Check to see whether the gnomon seems stable. If it isn't, bury its base in the soil beneath the gravel.)

10 To position the granite hour markers, you'll need to set aside a sunny afternoon and a sunny morning. At noon on the first day, set the noon marker on the gravel dial plate, locating it on an imaginary line extending from the point of the shadow that the gnomon is casting to the perimeter of the dial plate. At one o'clock in the afternoon, place another marker in the same fashion. Continue placing markers, every hour, on the hour, until the sun sets. You'll notice that the markers will run clockwise, away from the noon marker.

11 The next sunny morning, get up early and place the remaining markers, from sunrise to 11 A.M. These will run clockwise toward the noon marker.

SUNDIAL FACTS

The major difference between an accurate sundial and a watch or clock is that a sundial tells time as it actually is. A watch or clock, on the other hand, is designed to satisfy the human need for predictability. Because we'd like every day to pass in exactly twenty-four hours, we've invented a system in which every day does—it's called *Mean Time*. In reality, the time that passes between noon on one day and noon on another varies throughout the year. Also, "real" noon (when the sun is at its peak) in one part of a time zone can be different from "real" noon in another part of that time zone.

Until transportation improved during the Industrial Revolution, and until the telegraph was invented, people in a given region had no reason to care whether their local time matched the time in another region. (It made no difference to anyone that noon in one village might occur several minutes earlier or later than noon in another village several hundred miles away.) Establishing a timekeeping system that would be consistent internationally only became important when people could communicate quickly over long distances.

Sun Ornaments

Let sun ornaments cast dazzle, charm, and cheer about your yard. A variety of materials, from iridescent cloth to paper glassine to translucent colored plastic, cause special effects when struck by the sun. Nothing, however, reflects and refracts light like glass. You may worry that glass is too fragile for outdoor use, but, depending on its form, it's really quite durable. Its beauty and strength make glass ideal for backyard decor. Whether in the jeweled tones of a stained glass window or the romantic reflections of a Victorian gazing globe, glass has adorned gardens for centuries.

SHAPES AND FORMS

As you will see in the examples at far right, each type of glass treats light in a unique way. Whether glass will beam, gleam, glow, or glint also depends on the form it takes. Spherical shapes, such as the ones shown, will catch light from every possible angle, making them the most dramatic ornamental option. Just be sure to choose one made specifically for the garden, since most globes are made of blown glass, which is somewhat fragile.

For a playful effect, adorn your garden with versatile glass nuggets. Wrap them in wire (as we have, above) and dangle them from eaves or tree branches. Or, scatter them at your whim throughout flower beds, and catch their subtle wink as you wander past.

Sheets of glass, though flat, can be just as striking as the more three-dimensional shapes. Brightly colored panes may be cut, artfully arranged, and soldered together (by you or by a specialized glass worker) to create a lovely image that will brighten as the day does.

TYPES OF GLASS

Is all glass created equal? Hardly! In fact, a wide range of glass-making processes yields myriad colors, patterns, and effects. Art glass is usually divided into two categories: cathedrals and opalescents ("opals"). You are probably more familiar with cathedrals; these transparent glasses are often used in stained glass windows, dishware, and candleholders. Opals—less common but equally exquisite—are characterized by a crystallization process that renders them semi-opaque. Each type of glass varies in thickness depending on how heavily texturized it is. Described on the next page are some favorite cathedral and opalescent glasses.

TYPES OF GLASS

IRIDESCENT GLASS

Is it glass, or is it a soap bubble? We can thank a thin sprinkling of metallic salts for the colorful luster of iridescent glass, which will add a luminous glow to any garden.

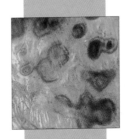

WATER GLASS

Boasting a sea of ripples and waves, water glass is appropriately named. When hot glass is stretched, it creates the undulating oceanic surface texture of water glass.

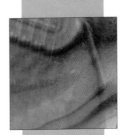

RING-MOTTLED GLASS

Ring-mottled glass will remind you of snakeskin, or maybe amoebas under a microscope. It is an opalescent glass that derives its name from opaque circular patterns on its surface.

STREAKY GLASS

What do you get when you cross one cathedral glass with another? The multicolored result is streaky glass, and it's formed by mixing—but not blending—cathedral glasses together.

GLUE-CHIP GLASS

You could almost mistake the delicate texture of this glass for winter frost. The look—very popular during the Art Nouveau period of late nineteenth century—is achieved by coating the surface with hot glue and then warming the glass slowly until fine particles flake away.

Shelter from the Sun

Most of the year, we revel in the warm glow of the sun. On a midsummer day, though, when that glow becomes a glare, your backyard can feel like an inferno. There's no need to hide inside with the air-conditioner blasting just when your garden is brimming with blooms! A variety of outdoor features serves double duty by adding style to your yard while providing shelter from the heat and harsh rays of the sun.

UMBRELLAS AND AWNINGS

Whether you attach an awning to the eaves above your patio or erect a large umbrella over a chaise longue, fabric is your ticket to instant shade. No formidable construction is involved, as with a gazebo, and you won't have to remember to water your awning as you would a planted pergola. On the contrary—be sure to pick a fabric that repels water, or mold will set in. Traditional canvas treated with a waterproofing agent is the most durable choice, while an open nylon weave wins points for affordability.

The longest lasting umbrellas will have sturdy frames made from heavy-gauge aluminum or hardwoods such as ash and mahogany. You can also extend the life of your umbrella by keeping it closed when it's not in use and storing it inside during inclement weather. Awnings can be permanent or retractable, and while the initial cost may seem high, you'll actually save money in the long run. Strategically placed, an awning can reduce the temperature of an adjacent room by 15° F (8° C) and consequently lower your air-conditioning costs. Fabrics for both awnings and umbrellas come in a variety of colors and patterns, giving you a great chance to add a splash of color to the backyard.

GAZEBOS

A gazebo is an actual garden room, an independent structure that offers not only shade, but quiet refuge from the spirited hubbub of backyard activity. Constructing a very complicated gazebo may call for the skills of a professional builder. But if you possess some basic carpentry skills, you can purchase a prefabricated gazebo kit and undertake the project on your own.

First, make sure your local building codes, zoning ordinances, and property deed allow the addition of a new building on your lot. Then, scout out a site for the gazebo. The ideal location will have good drainage and will offer surrounding foliage so that your gazebo will not appear unnaturally situated. If the gazebo is placed near your house, it is sure to become a common meeting ground, whereas a spot tucked away from commotion will provide privacy. Assess both options before you decide which will best suit your needs.

Ornamentally, you'll be faced with several choices throughout the course of construction. Shapes range from round to octagonal, from rectangular to three-sided. The best shape will complement your existing architecture. The same rule goes for trim, shingles, and other decorative aspects of the gazebo; for example, use bright red tile to top a gazebo next to your Spanish-style stucco home. Gazebo walls are most commonly made of screen or glass, but you may choose romantic trellises laced with fragrant blooms to enclose your space. For a more social atmosphere, or for a superior view of the garden, opt for no walls at all.

PERGOLAS

The most natural shade is that provided by an umbrella of leafy growth. A stately oak or maple would do the trick, but such trees take decades to cultivate. While you're waiting, why not spread a picnic beneath the pergola? A pergola, also called an arbor, is a simple frame fitted with a horizontal trellis overhead. When planted with thick, crawling vines, a pergola offers a ceiling of growth. Wood, brick, stone, and metal all make suitable pergola frames. Choose one that will accent, rather than detract from, your home. Wooden lattice, bamboo, or metal bars all make wonderful roofing; eager vines will scramble over any thin, sturdy material.

Candlelight in the Garden

Of course your garden is glorious when bathed in daylight, but what sets the mood after the sun goes down? How about a collection of strategically placed candles—housed, of course, in exquisite lanterns and luminaries? Flame may not be quite as bright as electrical lighting, but its soft and subtle glow is infinitely more ambient.

LANTERNS AND LUMINARIES

Candlelight has been around long enough to have generated countless forms and styles of candleholders—so many that they all seem to (if you'll pardon the expression) melt together. Tabletop, hanging, and pedestal candleholders are available in stained glass, wire mesh, handmade paper, and a host of other materials. These days,

we light candles for mood more than anything, so choose a style that suits your fancy and affects the atmosphere in subtle but sure ways.

Old-fashioned kerosene lanterns are a tried and true light source. Most lanterns are characterized by the shape of their globe. The hurricane lantern is named such for good reason; its especially bulbous globe keeps the flame lit

during even the most blustery evenings. Shop antique stores for old-timey miner's lanterns, whose globes feature reflective backing for brighter light.

Torches, too, use combustible fuel. The ever-popular tiki torch (far left) features a fuel well perched on a long pole; stake it anywhere to shed a festive light on backyard cookouts and soirees. The spherical Toledo torch (near left) rights itself immediately when tipped and features a nearly windproof flame.

CREATIVE CANDLEHOLDERS

Why not have some fun with your outdoor lighting scheme? Making your own candleholders is a great way to personalize your backyard decor in practically no time. Remember, though, to take extra measures to ensure that your inspired methods are safe ones. Let the following ideas guide you.

■ Punch a decorative pattern of holes into the side of an aluminum watering can. Place a lit votive within and then set the can in an unassuming nook in your garden.

■ Make your own paper luminary by bending a length of chicken wire into an open-ended square. Then, soak pre-sized paper in non-toxic decoupage glue and plaster it around the chicken wire. You'll be suprised at the lovely results of your own efforts!

■ For a sturdy base with architectural overtones, cut a banister head or length of deck railing to the desired height. Pierce the center with a single

CANDLES: A CRASH COURSE

Familiarize yourself with the various types of candles available and you'll be able to choose the best ones to light up your garden. First of all, the type of wax that constitutes a candle—usually either beeswax or paraffin—largely determines how it burns. Beeswax is an all-natural material that burns clean and sweet-smelling. Candles made from beeswax are the choice of most purists, but they do have one drawback: Their tendency to drip. In contrast, paraffin is a practical and convenient alternative. Derived from petroleum, its additives prevent excessive drips. Paraffin is odorless, has a glossy finish, and can be spiked with citronella to keep bugs at bay.

Both beeswax and paraffin come in a wide assortment of shapes and sizes. Pictured here are some of the most useful varieties (clockwise from upper left): floating candles, tapers, pillars, and tea lights.

nail, and impale a pillar candle—what a grand effect!

■ Small mounds of slightly hardened polymer clay are excellent bastions for tapers or tea lights. Unadorned, they hold an air of simplicity. For a bit of pizazz, embed them with rhinestones or colorful bits of glass.

SAFETY BY CANDLELIGHT

Your garden is chock-full of flammable material, especially in the autumn and winter months, when leaves and grasses dry out. Naturally, you must

exercise reasonable caution when using candles in an outdoor setting. Always set candles and candleholders on a steady surface that's shielded from the wind and well out of reach of surrounding foliage. Each time you light your garden torches, make sure they're staked deeply into the ground. Take extra care with paper luminaries, allowing plenty of space between the wick and the paper; choose chimney-style paper luminaries over globe styles, which can trap heat. Finally, never leave flame unattended.

Ornamental Ice Luminary

Have you ever noticed how much more we appreciate what we know won't last? Maybe it's the fleeting nature of this ice luminary—sorry, but it *will* eventually melt—that gives it its beauty. Whatever the case, it's sure to be a exquisite addition to your backyard, either nestled into a snowy landscape or used to cool off a scorching summer's day. We used colorful pansies to offset the ice, but you may substitute berries or foliage. Juniper, holly, eucalyptus and cranberry hold up particularly well under ice.

MATERIALS & TOOLS

- Cardboard box
- Small plastic garbage bag
- Tacks or pins
- Tin can
- Crushed or chopped ice
- Large spoon
- Gravel, one handful
- Flowers, berries, or foliage of your choosing
- Pencil or chopstick
- Water
- Candle

TIP

- Your luminary can be almost any size you choose, but select your materials with this in mind: The cardboard box must be smaller than your freezer, the tin can must be smaller than the cardboard box, and the candle that you use must be smaller than the tin can.

Instructions

1 First, find a cardboard box that's the same size as the luminary you intend to make. Line the box with a small plastic garbage bag. Smooth out any wrinkles that could create bumps and ridges in the sides of the luminary (unless, of course, you'd like a textured look). Tack or pin the bag to the corners of each cardboard panel to keep it from shifting while you work.

2 Hold the tin can in the center of the box so that the top of the can is aligned with the rim of the box. Add ice to the area beneath the can so that the can eventually rests on the cubes. Fill the can with gravel to help it stay put until you've finished working.

3 Begin slipping the flowers, berries, or foliage into the nooks and crannies of the ice. Use a pencil or chopstick to nudge and poke them into the right spot.

4 Pour just enough water into the plastic-lined box to cover the ice. Scoop another layer of ice (several inches thick) onto the previous layer. Add more flowers or berries as desired before pouring in more water.

5 Continue in this fashion until the iced water meets the rim of the box. If flowers or berries begin to float away, anchor them with a spoonful of ice.

6 Freeze the luminary for 24 to 36 hours. When you're certain that it's solid, begin unmolding your creation. Dump the rocks from the tin can, then fill the can with warm running water until you're able to loosen and remove it from the ice.

7 Rip the box and unwrap, peeling the plastic away from the ice as you do. Finally, place a candle in the hollow where the tin can was, strike a match, and enjoy the ethereal glow of your ice luminary!

Backyard Firebuilding

Gaze into a campfire, and memories will start to beckon: the smell of your first perfectly roasted marshmallow, the autumn clambake where you proposed to your spouse. Relive these memories—and create some new ones—in the welcoming glow of your own backyard.

When it comes to instant ambience, the flickering light, bewitching crackle, and woodsy scent of a fire are hard to beat. But this most primitive form of outdoor lighting is functional as well. With the proper equipment, you can use your fire to cook a sumptuous meal. And the smoke from the fire will keep mosquitoes and other pesky insects from dining on you and your guests! A number of products are now available that make it easy to escape from the technology-fueled world to the primitive comfort of an outdoor fire.

THE CHIMINEA

This new trend in outdoor stoves is actually ancient: The chiminea (also called a piña stove) was originally used by the Mayans for cooking. These days, the chimineas that garden centers import from Mexico are used primarily to decorate the garden. Throw a piñon log in the stove and it will also pleasantly perfume the air.

To use a chiminea, some preparation is involved. The outer surface is usually sealed by the manufacturer, but

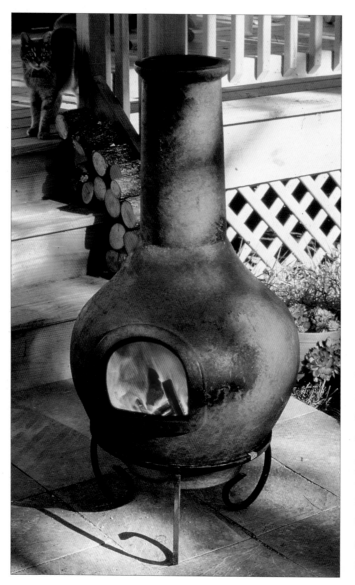

you will need to reapply a sealant (floor wax will do the trick) yearly. Also, fill the bottom of the chiminea with a layer of dry-washed sand to diffuse the heat of the fire. Most importantly, cure the inside of the stove by burning a series of five to ten small fires. When substantial soot has accumulated, you may begin to build slightly larger fires. If you skip this step and start a larger fire before soot has sealed your chiminea, it will very likely crack.

Because chimineas are made of clay—infamous for fragility—it's best to heed certain precautions. The greatest threat to your chiminea is a drastic temperature change, which can cause the clay to crack. This means that you should store the chiminea indoors during harsh winter weather. And never use lighter fluid in your chiminea; it encourages the fire to burn hot too quickly and also soaks into the clay, converting your chiminea into a decorative bomb. Finally, hardwoods such as mesquite burn too hot to be used in these stoves —stick to slower-burning fuel like the aforementioned piñon.

Investing in a few accessories will make your chiminea both safer and more convenient. For example, unless you set the stove on a fireproof surface such as stone or concrete, you'll need a cast-iron stand. A hinged fire screen that attaches to the stand is available for some models; this will catch flying sparks. A set of fire tools, including poker, shovel, and broom, will help you tend the fire. Finally, you will need a rain cap to keep water from entering the stove's chimney. You can purchase one from the manufacturer or just use a terra cotta saucer.

PORTABLE CAMPFIRES AND FIRE PITS

If you'd like a bigger blaze than a chiminea can handle, consider a portable campfire or a fire pit. A portable campfire is a highly utilitarian, aesthetically low-key way to have a fire right where you want it. Consisting of a round metal firebox topped with a detachable screen and propped on three legs, a portable campfire is a lightweight, no-frills alternative to the chiminea. Large enough to handle full size logs, most portable campfires come with optional grills for cooking.

A true backyard enthusiast may choose to clear out a permanent fire ring. A fire ring will accommodate a decisively larger fire than the portable options, which makes it a feasible source of heat in the cooler seasons. While you may have to sacrifice precious garden space, a fire pit is a feature that—properly supervised—your entire family can enjoy. To build your own backyard fire pit, follow our instructions on page 50.

Backyard Fire Safety

While fretting over strict safety measures may seem a nuisance, the simple fact is that fire is dangerous. All the ambience in the world is not worth having an out-of-control blaze put your property and well-being at risk. Many areas require suburban fire builders to apply for a permit before burning. Contact your local fire department to see if you need to obtain authorization; then take the following steps to ensure that your recreational fire is a safe one.

- Before lighting your fire, remove twigs, leaves, and all other flammable material within a three-foot radius of the fire site.
- Keep a safe distance of at least thirty feet from any trees or wooden structures.
- Never leave a fire unattended.
- Keep a shovel on hand for heaping dirt on overzealous blazes and a full pail of water nearby in case flames get out of control.
- Always be sure that you've completely extinguished your fire before leaving the site. When in doubt, rake through the ashes in search of glowing embers.

Backyard Fire Ring

If you want to enjoy fire the good old-fashioned way, you will find a fire ring to be a fine alternative to commercial outdoor fireplaces. With the approval of your local fire department, a well planned fire pit will allow you to host a backyard campfire sing-along at your whim. This simple design relies on readily available materials and minimal sweat and labor, as you'll find in the list and instructions below.

MATERIALS & TOOLS

- 3 cups flour
- 15 or so large stones
- 25 fist-sized stones
- Gravel (1 wheelbarrow load)
- Dry-washed sand (20-pound bag)
- Spade
- Hoe
- Rounded digging shovel
- Metal rake

TIP

- Fire pit regulations will vary depending on where you live. While the plan for this ring adheres to the requirements of many towns, yours may be different. A member of your local fire department should be happy to look over these instructions and make suggestions for modification specific to your area (the pit shown here, for example, was constructed in an asymmetrical shape to better suit the lay of the land).

Instructions

1 Select a site for your fire ring, ideally at least 30' from the nearest tree lines or other significant vegetation. This should give you distance from root growth and overhanging branches, both highly flammable.

2 Strip a patch of land roughly 10' in diameter, removing all signs of growth. Stripping grass is easiest if you use your spade to cut and lift the sod, then roll it away. Loosen any remaining roots with a hoe and scrape away all traces of vegetation. These can go into your compost pile.

3 In the approximate center of the bare patch, use flour to sketch out a rough circle about 3' across; the fire will burn here.

4 Three and a half feet from the flour drawing, make another circle concentric to the one you've just drafted. This will be the edge of your fire ring (the remaining 3½' constitutes a buffer zone for safety).

5 Using the digging shovel, begin removing dirt from the innermost circle. This hole should be deeper in the center than around the edges, the center being no more than 8" deep.

6 Line the shallow hole with the fist-sized rocks. These will provide a **fuel break** that prevents fire from spreading, and they will also allow you to shovel out spent ashes without accidentally removing soil.

7 Rim the rock bed with a ground-level ring of large stones, positioning them as close together as possible. If the stones seem wobbly, you may dig small ruts to stabilize them.

8 Use the rake to spread a layer of gravel 3" to 4" thick around the fire ring. Extend the gravel all the way to the outer circle you've drawn; this will reinforce the fuel break that the larger stones provide.

FIREBUILDING BASICS

In a single lifetime, how many books of matches do we waste trying to spark hopeless piles of wood meant to be campfires? And how many strong, bright blazes have risen from the tinder, only to peter out before the larger logs manage to catch? Building and tending a fire is inarguably an art—one that's lost on most modern suburbanites.

Firebuilding starts with a healthy stack of materials for burning. You'll need four basic types of fuel: Tinder (dry, lightweight material such as newspaper and dried leaves) burns quickly and eventually ignites the kindling; kindling is somewhat more substantial and consists of small twigs; sticks form the framework that allows a good campfire to freely burn; and wood is the hefty stuff that anchors the blaze.

Building these materials into a structure that lets the flame spread from smaller to larger fuel while providing adequate ventilation is the key to a successful fire. To begin, collect a large handful of tinder and ball it into a compact pile. Then use the kindling to form a tepee around the tinder. Next, stack the larger sticks log-cabin style around the tepee, creating a four-walled "house" slightly taller than the tepee. The most common mistake at this stage is to place the sticks so close together that air cannot flow through. Just remember, a breathing fire is a blazing fire. Now use three heavy logs to form an "H"—one log on each of two sides of the house, and one log crossed over the top.

Break out your matchbook; it's time to make some sparks. Shield the match from the wind and light the tinder in the very center of the pile. Kneeling down and blowing deeply and steadily into the base of the blaze will help fan the fire. When you are certain that the heavier logs are burning, slowly add more fuel.

Electrical Outdoor Lighting

By the time you plow through rush hour traffic and clear the dinner dishes, the plantings you've tended for so many weeks will likely be lost in the dark. Especially in the fall and winter, when daylight is more limited, the endless span of pitch-black viewed from a picture window or the edge of the patio can be disappointing. You might want to enjoy the deep red roses climbing up your new trellis or, on a more practical note, see the path to the compost heap as you step into the night with a bucket of vegetable scraps. Fortunately, electrical outdoor lighting systems have evolved that make it easier to linger a little longer in the garden.

REASONS FOR LIGHTING

Like just about every other aspect of garden design, it pays to put your enthusiasm on hold and do some planning before running out to buy

light fixtures or even hiring an expert to install lights. First, stop and think about all the different reasons for lighting your yard. You may wish to improve the safety and security of your home after dark. Strategically placed lights can make it easier for family and friends to climb steps or traverse narrow paths to get to your front door while at the same time discouraging intruders. Then again, perhaps your main objective is not security but the ability to spend more time enjoying your deck or patio in the cool evening hours. You may have a water feature that would look magical in the right light or an oak tree that could be magnificent when lit.

Another reason for outdoor lighting is to improve the view from inside the house. Many contemporary homes feature large expanses of glass, which bring the outdoors in while the sun shines. Unfortunately at night, all of those large windows and glass doors become black mirrors that can make occupants feel claustrophobic. When you light features of the outdoor landscape, the glass seems to disappear and the indoors suddenly feels larger.

Of course, you don't need to choose just one reason to add outdoor lighting, but it does help to prioritize your purposes. Then, with a little advanced planning, you can develop a lighting scheme that will accomplish all of your goals with the least amount of effort, expense, and disruption of established plantings.

TYPES OF LIGHTING SYSTEMS

In the past, installing electrical outdoor lighting was an expensive, time-consuming task best left to professionals. Now, technology offers options to the homeowner, specifically between low-voltage and standard-voltage systems.

The low-voltage lighting system is a blessing to the weekend gardener. The fixtures are easy to install and easy to relocate, so they can be adjusted to highlight the gems of each season and also adjusted as your garden grows and changes over the years. Unlike standard-voltage systems, they need not be mounted on a junction box or have their cables buried deep beneath the ground. For this reason, low-voltage installations cause much less disturbance amongst plantings, which is important considering the care and cultivation that you have invested in your garden.

Another advantage of low-voltage lighting is that the fixtures tend to be small, so they are easily hidden from view. This is definitely a case where you will get what you pay for, in terms of both light quality and durability. Get the best fixtures you can afford, and you'll save money in the long run on operating and replacement costs. The light from quality low-voltage fixtures is actually a sharper, more focused light than that from most standard-volt fixtures.

One common problem with poorly made low-voltage lighting systems is "dimming"—a decrease in light output from the last lights on a cable due to voltage drop. If you have a very large yard to light, you might want to consider investing in a standard-voltage system. With these lighting systems, fixtures must be mounted on an electrical junction box, and the cables must be buried at least 12 inches below grade. Standard lighting systems sometimes bear a hefty price tag and often require a special permit before they can be installed. Electricity is not something to be tinkered with—the complexities of standard-voltage systems mandate the services of a licensed electrician familiar with local codes. (In some locations, even low-voltage systems must meet codes.)

ORNAMENTAL GARDEN LIGHTING

Now that you know the types of outdoor lighting available, how will you use that lighting to maximize the aesthetic potential of your garden? As with any decorating venture, orchestrating outdoor lighting demands some sense of design. Too much light will look garish, while many scattered bright spots will make your backyard look like a circus ring. Your best bet is to choose one area to underscore with strong light, then accentuate with softer lights nearby. In doing so, you create emphasis and depth in your nightscape. Familiarizing yourself with the following three basic techniques will help you get started.

Moonlighting (also called down-lighting) usually involves floodlights

Sidelighting

need special fixtures fitted with water-proof, gasketed lenses for uplighting.

Finally, *sidelighting* is a technique used to exaggerate the texture of lit objects and to create a fine silhouette on a surface in the background.

Don't let all this design-speak intimidate you! Experimenting with outdoor lighting can be fun, and you'll be surprised at the effects you create.

The hardest part about lighting your outdoors may be reining yourself in. You're not trying to make it look like daylight out there—the nighttime garden has its own special magic. Think of it as an opportunity to hide your horticultural disappointments under the cloak of darkness, while putting a spotlight on your stars.

poised high in trees or on structures and aimed downward. Because we are accustomed to seeing the moon gleam down from above, downlighting produces natural-looking effects. When projected through an intricate tangle of branches, downlights create a lacy pattern on the ground below.

Uplighting accentuates a particular garden feature from the ground up. This technique creates backyard drama by emphasizing the sculptural quality of plants, especially trees. With uplighting, light particles emanate into the air rather than hit a hard background surface. The result is a soft glow, rather than a defined shadow, in the garden. Because light normally comes from above, not below, the effect is somewhat unnatural. Use uplighting sparingly to create a few dramatic focal points in the garden. Note that you'll

Uplighting

GARDEN ART AND WHIMSY

light

Left: Sundials come in many shapes and forms, but few so inventive as this one. The saucer of water not only reflects the shadow of the gnomon and tells time, it also serves as a birdbath. Exquisitely-wrought ornamental detail adds visual interest to the piece.

Right: Everyone's favorite summertime bug, the firefly, glows year-round with this unusual outdoor lantern. Look for lighting fixtures that appeal to your own sense of style and dress up your garden in a flash.

Above: When Jack Frost blows into your once-flourishing garden, don't be disheartened. Work *with* the weather, not against it. String up an empty trellis with festive lights to create a hopeful glow in a bleak landscape.

Below: Dramatically draped canvas and hand-made crowning ornaments offer unexpected grace to an otherwise ordinary pergola at Penland School of Craft. What's more, the wide dips in the tightly woven fabric form hammocks that conveniently accommodate several lounging students at once!

Right: The Victorian gazing globe has been a standard in gardens across the world for ages. This version, a slightly modern twist on the antique ornament, boasts a particularly loud color that brightens this overcast day.

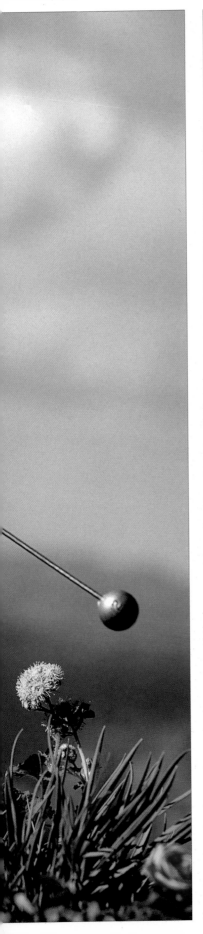

air

Our planet hosts about two hundred times more earth than sky; the air we breathe amounts to little more than a whisper. But *ah,* what a difference that broad stretch of sky makes when you step out into your backyard.

Celebrate the sweet, fresh air with whimsical backyard gadgets that spin, dance, and sing in the wind. Wind toys can be both fun and functional—stake a colorful collection of pinwheels throughout a terraced hillside, or build your own weather vane following the instructions provided in these pages. Next, get a little lift with swings guaranteed to send kids of all ages soaring, monkey around in your own treehouse hideaway, or just stretch out in a gently rocking hammock.

As you're relaxing, dream of an airborne existence while enjoying a little birdwatching. In these pages, you'll find ways to attract birds into a backyard abode they'll never want to leave. Use our detailed guide to build a basic birdhouse, and follow our steps to shroud your birdbath in a trellis covered with their favorite berries. So set that trowel down, look up, and find countless ways to resuscitate your outdoor living space!

Weather Vanes and Wind Socks

If you think that an accurate weather report is only available on your television screen, then think again. Would you believe that a glance out the window at a wind sock or weather vane might yield similar results? The world's oldest forecasters come in a wide and wonderful array of styles and forms—one of which is sure to complement your outdoor setting. Like the wind toys featured on pages 64 and 65, socks and vanes boast a whimsical quality that's truly irresistable. What's more, because they allow you to read the strength and direction of an oncoming bout of weather, they are undeniably practical.

WEATHER VANES

Ancient Greece stakes claim to many inventions still useful in the modern world, not the least of which is the weather vane. The first in history topped the peak of the Tower of Winds in Athens, circa 48 B.C. You needn't have so stately a structure on which to

perch your vane; any sturdy stake or fence post will do.

Several parts compose the weather vane. The finial, or crowning ornament, is attached to a long metal rod. The rod fits into a fixed hollow bushing, where the directionals (usually just "North" and "South") are indicated. When a breeze blows, the finial catches it like a sail and turns it away from the wind.

While styles vary wildly, most weather vanes can be placed into one of five categories. The simplest type of vane is an arrow—just a point and fletching attached to a horizontal tube. More intricately wrought arrows are often called "scrolls" because of their extensive detail. Banner-style vanes are fashioned after medieval pennants and include a simple point in the front and a wide, flag-like area in the back. Silhouettes have remained the most popular style of weather vane and have taken on a range of shapes and forms over the years. Used for centuries by everyone from European guildsmen to colonial farmers, silhouette vanes are also the easiest to make—as we've illustrated on page 62.

Swell-bodied vanes (pictured at left) and full-bodied vanes round out the range of styles. Beware—as exquisite as these three-dimensional designs are, they are also usually the most complicated to make since they require a certain amount of familiarity with sculptural techniques.

If you favor a handmade look, you can fashion your own vane from our pattern on page 63 or have a blacksmith hammer out a custom design just for you. Consider a sailboat if you've spent time at sea, for example, or a floral pattern if you treasure your green thumb. You may also find ready-made vanes at antique, farm supply, or specialty home decor stores.

WIND SOCKS

Wind socks—those silky tubes of fabric so treasured by aviation buffs—are a bit younger than weather vanes, but

WINDMILLS

The romance of the windmill is undeniable. Envision its form towering towards a clear sky, its slow, heavy, blades knifing the air in steady strokes. From the tenth century windmills of Persia to the more recent European post mill, windmills have remained a cornerstone of technological advancement. While the first windmills were used to grind grain and pump water, contemporary versions generate electricity as well.

Though your backyard is certainly no place for a classic Dutch grinding mill, wind toys that mimic its motion are widely available at garden supply stores and roadside folk art booths. Pay homage to this time-honored technology with a small-scale model, such as the one pictured here, in your garden.

every bit as useful. Around the turn of the century, after the Wright brothers set the flying craze into motion, discerning wind direction became more vital than ever before. As man soared higher and higher, brightly colored wind socks fluttered below to indicate the best landing direction. Your backyard is likely no airfield, but you'll still relish the sight of a decorative cloth sailing in the breeze—especially if it's predicting a week's worth of sunbathing weather. Since their early debut, wind socks have evolved quite a bit, sometimes ebbing from their utilitarian origins in favor of flashy, kite-like designs. These days, you'll find wind socks bearing a host of themes including animals, flowers, and other novelty shapes and emblems. The lily pictured at left will bloom year round!

Pointing Retriever Wind Vane

Just what is that noble labrador pointing at, anyway? A sassy cat sauntering by? A fat pheasant, newly flushed from the brush? Neither one. This fine canine, carved in a classic silhouette style, is pointing the wind. We've streamlined our vane by omitting the directionals. If you can't remember which way is which in your backyard, consider lettering N, S, E, and W on the four sides of the post and orient it accordingly.

MATERIALS & TOOLS

- Pencil
- Scissors
- Tape measure
- Straight edge
- Jigsaw or coping saw
- Drill
- ¼" and ⅜" drill bits
- Wood chisel
- Hammer
- One piece of scrap wood, at least 1" thick
- One ¼" metal rod, cut to 3" (Most hardware stores carry smooth rods 2' and 3' long. A hack saw works well for cutting the rod to size.)
- One ⅜"-outside diameter brass bushing, 1" long
- Sandpaper
- Exterior wood glue
- Exterior paints or stains

TIP

- Don't feel bound to use our design! If your pooch happens to be a poodle, dalmatian, or any other lovable creature, tell it to sit, stay, and pose while you draw a pattern of your own.

CUTTING LIST

DESCRIPTION	QTY.	MATERIAL
Retriever	1	10" x 20" x ¼" exterior-grade plywood
Arrow	1	1 x 4 x 28" pine, spruce, or fir
Stand (optional)	1	6 x 6 x 7½" pressure-treated post

Instructions

1 To create the cutting patterns for the dog and the arrow, photocopy the illustration, enlarging it to the dimension provided.

2 Cut out the paper patterns, and then trace the outline of the dog onto ¼"-thick plywood and the arrow onto the 1 x 4" pine, spruce, or fir.

3 Cut out the dog and the arrow with a jigsaw; then smooth all their edges by sanding them well.

4 Mark two points on the top of the arrow, one 7" and another 15" back from the arrow's point. Use a wood chisel to hollow two ½"-deep, 1¼"-long grooves starting at the marked points; the lab's feet will fit into these grooves.

5 Measure 7½" back from the arrow's point and use a ¼" drill bit to bore a 1"-deep hole in the bottom of the arrow (this hole may intersect one of the ¼"-long grooves).

6 Squirt a few drops of the exterior wood glue into the grooves and set the dog's feet in place. Then put a little glue in the hole in the bottom of the arrow and insert the 3" piece of smooth rod.

7 With a ⅜" bit, bore a 1"-deep hole in the center top of the pressure-treated post.

8 Position the brass bushing against the hole in the pressure-treated post. Place the piece of scrap wood on top of the bushing. Tamp the bushing into the hole by tapping a hammer against the scrap wood. (Hammering directly against the bushing might warp the metal and prevent the smooth rod from fitting correctly.)

9 Finish all the wooden pieces with exterior paint or stain and let them dry.

10 Insert the bottom end of the smooth rod into the brass bushing; then let that puppy catch some wind!

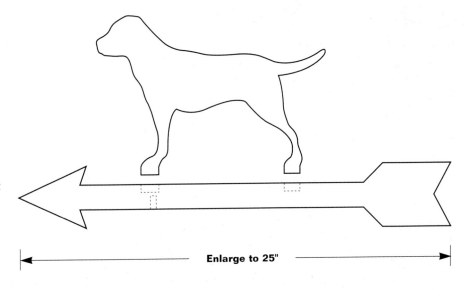

Enlarge to 25"

Wind Toys

As gardeners, we spend so much time hunched over in the dirt that we tend to forget about the skies above. Still, we know the therapeutic value of a fresh breeze and how a little wind can (literally) transform the atmosphere of a garden. Just think of that light zephyr that breathes life into a relaxing evening on the patio, or the strong gust that revives a dull summer day. Make the most of the wind that sweeps through your backyard by assembling a menagerie of spinning, singing ornaments.

SPINNERS

The heartfelt glee that a simple drugstore pinwheel provides is proof-positive of the inspired effects of wind toys.

The first pinwheel—a play model of the more hardworking windmill—was born in China sometime in the fifteenth century. You can find contemporary outdoor pinwheels at garden shops, or fashion your own using thin sheets of colored plastic (available at craft-supply stores) and wooden dowels, as is shown below.

Soon after their innovation, pinwheels evolved to include a host of styles, and *whyrlegyge* was used to describe any wind toy. Today, the word *whirligig* specifies one of two types of wind-driven knickknacks. Winged (or arm-waving) whirligigs have stationary bodies with wings or arms spinning on either side. Mechanical whirligigs are more complex: A propeller catches the

wind and drives a cam, gear, or wheel into motion. Through the ages, the ingenuity of whirligig crafters has known no bounds; the creative and complex designs often feature three or four levels of activity. Traditionally hand-whittled, whirligigs run the gamut, from rustic to contemporary, playful to political.

CHIMES AND MOBILES

Whether a rustling in the leaves or a quaking in the grass, when the wind blows, nature sings. For that matter, nature "sings" through the cracks in your windows on a stormy winter's night. If wind can transform these ordinary features into instruments—

however primitive—then almost any assembly of seemingly banal objects can relay a melody. Homemade chimes can be had with just a raid of your backyard shed: Mismatched silverware, keyring castoffs, colorful ceramic shards, or a handful of nuts and bolts can (when properly engineered) make marvelous music. Of course, there's no telling how harmonic their sounds will actually be. For traditionally tuned chimes, shop your local garden center, or follow our detailed instructions on page 66.

Mobiles—the wind chime's silent partner—can also be concocted from everyday articles (or store-bought if you'd prefer). Elegant in their form, ethereal in their soaring motion, mobiles are the perfect way to add a bit of grace and refinement to your garden. Collect an assortment of small, colorful toys and suspend them from a simple frame, string together several strands of beads and baubles, or bend wire into a sculptural shape that whirls and winds in the sky.

BANNERS, FLAGS, AND STREAMERS

The whoosh of a great wind will transfigure that banner, flag, or streamer hanging from your eaves; what was once a serene swath of color takes on a whipping, twisting life of its own. As fabrics go, silk best carries the breeze: its light weight and smooth surface offer little resistance to the wind.

A variety of fabric treatments widens your options; for example, batik is a method of wax-resist that yields layers and layers of pattern and color. Embroidered fabric offers interesting textures, while applique treatments result in a piecemeal design reminiscent of traditional quilting. All may be purchased at garden specialty stores. If you do decide to make your own banner or flag, be sure to tie together any leftover fabric scraps and attach them to a garden stake for instant streamers!

Aeolian Harps

*...Methinks, it should
    have been impossible
Not to love all things in a
    World like this
Where e'en the Breezes
    of the simple Air
Possess the power and
    Spirit of Melody!*

—Samuel Taylor Coleridge

Suffice it to say, nature is a talented songstress. When she sends her breath out over the malleable strings of the aeolian harp, you'll never hear the same tune twice. Depending on the mood of the skies, results can range from harmonious and melodic to eerie and dissonant. Named for the Greek god of the wind, Aeolus, this harp (also called a wind lyre) is one of the oldest musical instruments known to man. The instrument consists of 16 monofilament strings stretched loosely across an open wooden box. The strings are of equal length but varying diameters, all tuned in unison to the same note. When air moves through the box, the pitch that resonates is dependent entirely on wind velocity. Placing one of these ancient treasures in an open window spreads a hypnotic, shimmering sound that you'll hear indoors and out.

Arts and Crafts Wind Chime

Carrying a tune is easy when you let nature do the work for you! With a quick trip to the hardware store and a few hours of free time, you can easily drown out the agitating buzz of a Saturday morning mower, the incessant bark of a neighbor's yipping dog, or the hum of traffic on a nearby highway. What's more, the contrasting metals used in this wind chime make it look as good as it sounds.

MATERIALS & TOOLS

- 7' length of ½" copper tubing
- Vise
- Tape measure
- Hacksaw
- Half-round file
- Marking pen
- Electric drill and ¹⁄₁₆" bit
- 12" x 12" x ¾" cedar
- Compass
- Jigsaw
- ½"-wide .025 copper, 30" long
- 5" x 5" sheet of .025 copper
- Tin snips
- Awl
- Hammer
- Brass upholstery tacks
- ½" metal split ring
- Spool of monofilament (fishing line)
- Decorative brass-plated beads
- Scissors
- Rubber Cement

TIPS

- If you have a sheet metal shop in your town, ask if you can look through their scrap pile for the copper. Most shops have plenty of scrap that they will sell cheaply or even just give you!
- When you're ready to attach the tubes to the top of the chimes, remember that while aligning the top ends of the tubes may appeal to your visual sense, it isn't crucial to the creation of functional chimes.

Instructions

1 Secure the tubing in your vise and use a hacksaw to cut it to three 12" lengths and three 14" lengths, angling one end of each piece at 45°. Smooth any jagged edges with the flat side of the file.

2 Measure and mark two points on each tube, one point 1½" from the straight edge and one directly opposite the first. Drill a hole at each of those points.

3 Use a compass to draw two circles on the scrap of cedar, one 5" across and one 2½" across. Cut out the circles with a jigsaw and sand the rough edges away.

4 Measure and mark six equidistant points on the top side of the 5" circle of wood, each ¼" from the edge. Drill a hole through the wood at each point as well as one hole through the center of the circle. While you're at it, drill a hole in the center of the smaller circle of wood.

5 Use your tin snips to cut a piece of copper from the ½" strip that's 17" long. Wrap the copper around the edge of the 5" circle and overlap the ends. Use a marking pen to indicate on the strip where the first upholstery tack will be placed.

6 With your awl, make a hole at the marked point that pierces both layers of copper. Now, postion a tack in the hole and hammer it into the edge of the circle. Continue to space tacks around the edge of the circle, hammering them in one at a time. (Be sure that you're placing the tacks between the holes you've drilled in the wood. You don't want to block those holes with the ends of the tacks.)

7 Cut another piece of copper measuring 9" long. With this shorter strip of metal, repeat steps 5 and 6, this time using the smaller circle.

8 Cut a 3'-long piece of monofilament and tie it to the metal split ring. Thread the free end down through one of the holes on the edge of the 5" circle, back up through a neighboring hole, through the split ring, and back down through the next closest hole. Continue until the monofilament comes up through the last hole; then tie the free end to the split ring. This threading pattern will allow the chimes to hang level.

9 Cut six lengths of monofilament, each 16" long. Take one length and thread it through the holes of one of the tubes. Bring one end of the monofilament up through a hole in the 5" circle and the other end up through an adjacent hole, and tie the two ends of the monofilament with a secure knot. Repeat this process for each of the remaining five tubes.

10 When all of the tubes are in place, cut off the excess monofilament and slide each knot down in a hole to conceal and protect it. Hang your wind chime on a nail at a comfortable working height to make the following step easier.

11 Cut a 30" length of monofilament and tie one end to the split ring. Maneuver the monofilament through the center hole and slide a bead and then the 2½" circle onto the monofilament. Follow the circle with a second bead and make a knot. The beaded assembly should hang roughly in the center of the tubes.

12 Enlarge the shield pattern and trace it onto a piece of paper. Use rubber cement to adhere the paper pattern to the 5" x 5" copper sheeting. Cut out the shield shape with tin snips and file the jagged edges until they are smooth.

13 Drill a hole in the top of the shield as indicated by the pattern shown, and tie the shape to the end of the monofilament.

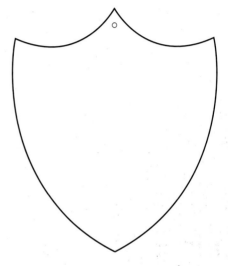

Swings

Feeling a little too grounded? Maybe all you need is a little liftoff—Tarzan-style. Nothing is more liberating than hurtling headlong into the wind. If a more sedate swing is what you have in mind, sit back and relax in a glider. Generations of Southerners—for whom centuries of gossip, courtship, war, and peace have risen and fallen to the gentle swaying of porch swings and gliders—swear by their therapeutic qualities. Whether recreational, functional, or both, swings and gliders are simple and well-deserved garden luxuries.

ROPE AND TIRE SWINGS

The simplest style of swing is the rope swing—just a strand of freedom dangling from a single point. What's unique about rope swings is that instead of just taking you back and forth like plank swings do, they spin, whirl, and twirl, too. Traditional rope swings are made from heavy hemp with a large knot at the free end to support the rider's feet. Hemp tends to chafe a bit, but it does offer a superior grip. Most nylon ropes are slightly more comfortable to grasp, but they're

also more difficult to hang on to, as nylon tends to be slippery. Nylon rope works well if you're planning on creating a more evolved and secure version of the rope swing—one that features a wooden disk for the rider to sit or stand on as he or she grips the rope.

Tire swings usually fall into the rope-swing category as well and are remarkably easy to make. Just hang a tire by attaching a rope to it. (Instructions for attaching ropes securely are provided on page 71.)

PENDULUM SWINGS AND GLIDERS

Pendulum-style swings may not take you around the world, but their almost 180-degree thrust can provide plenty of excitement. A plank swing like the one featured on page 70 is a breeze to build and can be safer than the more primitive rope swings. This type of swing can offer a gentle ride or a wild one, depending on the length of rope you use—and the courage you exhibit.

A more subtle way to stay in motion is to integrate a swing or glider into your garden furniture collection. The porch swing is a timeless classic, but make sure that the ceiling of your porch is stable enough for safe attach-

ment. If you aren't blessed with a sturdy porch ceiling, consider hanging the same style of swing from a freestanding A-frame structure, as shown in the photo to the right. A glider such as the one shown on the opposite page is also a good alternative. This smooth-riding piece of furniture is a cross between a rocking chair and a swing, but its gentle back-and-forth motion can be even more relaxing. The hammock, another universal source of rest and recuperation, has a history that stretches back to ancient times, when a student of Socrates is rumored to have invented it. Since then, the hammock has inspired laziness in anyone snared by its net. (For detailed information on hammocks, see page 72.)

SAFE LAUNCHING

Before you go airborne, you'll need to start with a steady and secure launching point. Engineering a swing isn't difficult, but a vital step before the fun begins is to ensure passenger safety. Consider where to site your swing, keeping in mind the importance of a pleasant view and a soft landing. Examine the vegetation beneath your chosen site. Then bid it farewell, as it will inevitably be trampled if a swing is hung above it.

If you plan to hang your swing from a tree, choose a strong one—maple, oak, and ash work best. The branch you select should be alive, healthy, and at least six inches in diameter (or larger if the tree is a less hardy variety). Don't loop the rope around the branch; this common suspension method actually suffocates the limb, thereby posing a threat to the rider's safety. Instructions for safe attachment of swings are provided on the next two pages.

High-Flying Plank Swing

What is it about swings that's so captivating? Feeling your hair sweep back in the wind as you rise through the air? The rush of excitement as your feet leave the ground? The almost irresistible challenge of seeing just how high you can go? Throughout the ages, the basic plank swing has delighted passengers both young and old. From the open-air picnics of France to the religious festivals of India, this simple type of swing has played a starring role in cultures worldwide. And unlike many of the other "toys" you may remember from your childhood, swings are never outdated. Maybe that's because adults enjoy them just as much as children.

MATERIALS & TOOLS

- ¾" x 10" x 24" poplar
- Sandpaper
- Electric drill
- ¼" and ⁵⁄₁₆" drill bits
- ½" wrench
- Pliers
- Tape measure
- Sturdy ladder
- Tool apron
- Two ⅜" eyebolts
- Four ¼" eyebolts
- Four ¼" washers
- Four ¼" locknuts
- Six ¼" quick-link joints
- Eight ⅜" cable clips
- Two lengths of strong chain, each 18" long
- Two lengths of heavy nylon or oiled hemp rope
- Polyurethane sealer
- 3" paintbrush

TIPS

- The tree limb you select for your swing should be at least 6" in diameter.
- The lengths of the rope you use for this swing will depend on the height of the tree limb you choose. Cut these at least 18" longer than you think they need to be; you can always trim them later.

■ A safe way to attach ropes to a swing is to use devices known as cable clips. You'll find these at a hardware store. One warning here: Cable clips can loosen over time, so check and tighten them frequently!

Instructions

1 The 10" x 24" piece of poplar will serve as your swing seat. Measure and mark a point at each of its corners, 2" in from a short end and 2" in from a long edge.

2 Using the electric drill and the ¼" bit, drill a hole through the seat at each of the four marked points.

3 To smooth all the sharp edges on the seat, sand them thoroughly.

4 To preserve the wood from the elements, apply a couple of coats of polyurethane sealer, letting the first coat dry thoroughly before applying the next.

5 Insert a ¼" eyebolt into each hole in the seat, with the eye on the top face of the seat. Secure each bolt with a ¼" washer and locknut.

6 Attach a quick-link joint to each eyebolt. Then link the ends of each chain to the quick-link joints so that each chain runs from the front of the swing to the back.

7 Attach another quick-link joint to the center of each chain.

8 To attach the rope to the tree branch you've selected, set your ladder against the tree, and have a friend hold it steady. Put on your tool apron: You'll need to bring your drill, the ⁵⁄16" drill bit, a tape measure, the two ³⁄8" eyebolts, a pair of pliers, four cable clips, the wrench, and the two lengths of rope when you climb up the ladder. Take a good look at the illustration to the right before you make your ascent!

9 Measure 30" out from the trunk of the tree and drill a ⁵⁄16" hole in the bottom of the limb. Measure out another 20" and drill a second ⁵⁄16" hole, also in the bottom of the limb. Then insert an eyebolt into each hole, using the pliers to twist them in.

10 Slip one end of a length of rope through two cable clips, through one of the eyebolts in the branch, and back down through the cable clips. Adjust the clips, one beneath the other, so they face in opposite directions. Then use the wrench to tighten the nuts on the cable clips so they'll secure the rope firmly. Repeat to fasten the other rope to the second eyebolt.

11 Once you're back on the ground again, use the technique described in step 10 to attach the other ends of the rope to the quick-link joints on the swing-seat chains.

Hammocks

After a long walk behind a mower or a formidable bout with the weeds, you deserve nothing so much as to rest in the suspended cradle of a sweetly rocking hammock. Sources conflict on the origin of everyone's favorite backyard lair. However, we do know that leisure hounds across the globe—from Central America to the Greek Isles—have long championed the comfort, durability, and convenience of the hammock. You, too, will sing its praises after a lazy afternoon in its gentle embrace.

TYPES OF HAMMOCKS

Before outfitting your backyard with a hammock, survey the market to find a style that meets your needs. The first hammocks were woven from the pliable bark of trees like hamack (their namesake) or sisal; subsequently, sailors favored hemp hammocks. These days, you're more likely to find hammocks made of sturdy rope, string, or cloth.

Rope hammocks, which offer stretch and comfort without sacrificing durability, have a classic appeal. Often equipped with a horizontal stave at each end that "opens" it and exaggerates its girth, the rope hammock has a friendly, welcoming feel. Alternatively, the rope hammock may feature just one stave that connects the two ends and creates a hanging chair, as shown here. Though the wide weave

of the rope hammock is undeniably cozy, it may leave a waffle print on bare legs and arms. You can easily remedy this problem by spreading a lightweight blanket over the weave before you sprawl out for your nap.

The Mayan string hammock is not as prevalent in suburban backyards as the rope hammock, but for all its ease and affordability, it should be! Engineered by the same people who built

the Central American pyramids, the string hammock is no less impressive in its design. The string is soft against the skin (no waffling) but exceptionally strong due to the tight weave. Like rope hammocks, some stringed versions feature staves that spread the hammock out; those that do not are lightweight and highly portable, easily toted along on family beach trips or camping expeditions. Though the string used to make the Mayan hammock is fairly hefty, exposing it to sharp objects—even buttons and zippers—can inflict irreparable damage upon your hammock.

The third and final type of hammock available is made of cloth. These were popularized by the navy, whose seafaring bunks originally consisted of canvas hammocks. The actual comfort of a cloth hammock will depend on how much "give" or flex the material has; too much or not enough will leave you with sore, creaky joints (as if the marathon afternoon of yard work weren't enough!). Before purchasing a cloth hammock, give it a "test rest" to make sure it suits you.

USE AND MAINTENANCE

You may situate your hammock between any two solid, reliable points. Trees are ideal lashing posts if your backyard happens to have two that are 8 to 14 feet apart; otherwise, drive heavy stakes into the ground and secure them with cement. (Another option is to purchase a hammock stand, which come in wood or metal and can be stored in your garage or shed when not in use.)

When hanging the hammock, handle it by the ends to avoid tangling. Secure the ends of standard-sized hammocks at a height of six to eight feet (lower if small children will be clambering about). Now, make sure you have your hammock survival kit—plenty of reading material and a cooler stocked with your favorite beverage—at arm's length, and climb in. Ahhhhhhh.

Treehouses

Perching atop a tree isn't just for the birds. Humans have demonstrated a hunger for heights since ancient times, when the Roman emperor Caligula held banquets in the enormous limbs of a plane tree. During the Italian Renaissance, the Medici family held competitions to see who could build the grandest treehouse. Unfortunately, since those times, treehouses have been regarded largely as kids' stuff. Recently, however, they've undergone a renaissance of their own, gaining a foothold in contemporary alternative architecture. People live, work, and even vacation in treehouses and treehouse resorts. You may not want to go so far as to install a hot tub in the limbs of your backyard oak, but you don't have to stop at nailing a few flat boards to its branches. A little forethought will go a long way toward giving you a cozy, raised room with a view.

PLANNING YOUR TREEHOUSE

First, decide whether you'll build the house yourself (you'll need some basic construction experience if you do) or have someone else do it for you. Then decide what purpose your treehouse will serve. Who will use it? Will they eat, sleep, read, or play in it? Do you want to locate it conveniently close to your house or nestle it far away in a hidden corner of the yard?

Make sketches of both your dream palace and of realistic alternatives. Consult books on treehouses for inspiration, and use your sketches as you work toward a final design. With these sketches in mind, choose a tree in which to build. Maple, oak, and ash have the best reputations for strength and hardiness, but obviously your choices will be limited to what's grow-

ing in your backyard. The truth of the matter is that almost any type of tree of the right size can support a properly engineered structure. When in doubt, though, check with an arborist and an architect.

Once you've chosen a tree, determine the height at which you'll place the treehouse. This is a vital safety consideration: Walls erected at extreme heights in unprotected areas will act as sails that catch the wind, and will threaten the stability of the structure. And do you really want your small child climbing that high? Even if you plan to construct a simple platform-style structure, which will fare better than more complex designs at higher branch levels, proceed with caution.

Branch thickness is another important consideration. Locate the places on the tree where you'll need to fasten supports and measure the circumference at those points. Depending on the type of tree you've chosen, and the weight of the structure, look for branches at least eight to twelve inches in diameter. Ensure the safety of the future treehouse inhabitants by carefully considering these factors and by consulting a treehouse construction manual.

TREEHOUSES FOR KIDS

Your child, of course, needs a getaway as much as you do. Kids are rarely out of the range of watchful adult eyes, and treehouses are famed for the sense of privacy and refuge they offer. Very few activities offer children a better sense of ownership than involvement in the planning and building process. In a note to his carpenter, a president once scrawled "Please have this [treehouse] built. [My daughter] will help...To be placed as directed by her." Allowing children a role in the decision-making process and a hand in the construction will enhance their appreciation for the structure and the personal space that it provides—not to mention their carpentry skills!

LOFTY LIVING

All sorts of things that are fun to do inside are even more delightful when they take place up in the leafy canopy of a tree!

Napping Nook. Snuggling into the limbs of a century-old oak provides an unparalleled sense of sweet security. Whether you actually build a sleeping structure into your treehouse or just store a blanket and pillow up there, you'll sleep like a baby in your treetop retreat.

Studio. Do you have a secret yearning to try your hand as a painter? Is your child determined to master the tuba, but your family unable to tolerate one more note wailing through the house? No matter the art form, a treehouse can liberate the creative spirit while providing the solitude necessary for artistic endeavors.

Dining Perch. Whether the kids are having a tea party with their teddy bears or you're hosting dinner for that special someone, dining on high can be a special treat. Spread a picnic blanket and some cushions if floors are coarse, or consider adding a small table and a few chairs to your treehouse.

Reading Refuge. A good book always provides an escape for weary minds. Reading in a treehouse, however, will really send your imagination soaring. Try some of these great treehouse reads:

Baron in the Trees	**Italo Calvino**
Swiss Family Robinson	**Robert Louis Stevenson**
Walden	**Henry David Thoreau**
Meetings with Remarkable Trees	**Thomas Pakenham**

Birdhouses

You may already have a bird feeder, a birdbath, and an abundance of flora to encourage feathered folk to feast and flourish in your garden. Why not beckon the birds to stay awhile and raise a family? Imagine the delight of discovering a tiny pile of delicate eggs, the pleasure of seeing hatched nestlings, and the final excitement of watching the fledglings take flight on their wobbly wings. With a bit of inspiration and planning, you'll soon have your own backyard bird sanctuary.

About 80 species of North American birds are "cavity nesters" who find natural homes in the hollows of decaying trees (now in short supply due to logging practices). But you don't have to transplant a hollowed tree to your backyard—though some people actually have!—to invite their company. Many cavity nesters are easily attracted to conventional birdhouses, or nest houses, including bluebirds, chickadees, nuthatches, wrens, kestrels, and purple martins. Whether you choose to buy or build a house for nesting birds, you'll have the pleasure of sharing their family life while helping to protect and preserve bird populations whose natural habitats are increasingly threatened.

BUYING A BIRDHOUSE

Shopping for a birdhouse can be a lot like choosing your own house plan. A vast array of possible designs awaits you—from miniature barns, log cabins, and hollowed-out gourds to replicas of Frank Lloyd Wright homes. You'll find a wide variety of birdhouses at garden and hardware stores, at gift shops, and in mail-order catalogs.

The first step is to decide what kinds of birds you'd like to have as neighbors. The next is to select a house (or multiple houses) that will be safe and functional for your birds of choice. The dimensions of a birdhouse and the manner in which it's sited are important; each type of bird has its own requirements (see "Birdhouse Specifications" on page 79). The entrance hole, for example, should be large enough to admit the bird, but small enough to keep out unwanted guests. If you're limited to only one house, choose one with an entry hole 1½ inches in diameter; it will accommodate the greatest variety of birds.

Hardy houses made from well-insulated materials will protect birds and their eggs from extreme heat and cold. Wood is always a reliable choice; however, some of the newer composite materials offer comparable quality. You'll also find houses made of glazed ceramic, plastic, and terra-cotta. With the exception of aluminum martin houses, avoid metal birdhouses. Even a wooden house with a metal roof will overheat in direct sun. Also avoid other materials that might be harmful to birds, such as lead-based paint and creosote- or pressure-treated lumber. And keep in mind that although houses with authentic architectural appeal and colorful paint jobs make delightful garden decorations, they're often more fanciful than functional.

To protect the house (and the birds) from rain and to prevent water damage, make sure the front edge of the roof overhangs the entrance hole by at least two inches, and that the sides are nailed to the edges of the floor rather than to its top. Holes or slits in the bottom of the house will allow for proper drainage and help prevent rotting caused by accumulated water. Birdhouses should also have ventilation holes or slits. If your favorite house lacks these, either drill two ⅝-inch-diameter holes or cut a horizontal slit near the top of each side wall.

You'd think that perches on bird-houses would always be desirable features, as they are on feeders. Not true! Cavity-nesting birds don't usually need them, and the only birds that prefer them are house sparrows and European starlings—two species that fall into the "unwanted guest" category.

You'll also want to choose a house that's easy to clean after each nesting. A hinged side or roof (not the bottom) works best, but be sure to keep the hinged section securely closed. Crafty raccoons are persistent predators, and may figure out how to unlatch hook-and-eye fasteners.

BUILDING A BIRDHOUSE

If you'd like to try your hand at build-ing your own birdhouse, your best bet is to begin with a simple project, such as the bluebird house featured on page 80. If you're not quite ready to tackle building a house from scratch, try transforming an ordinary birdhouse into a whimsical work of garden art with a few creative touches of your own. Let your imagination lead the way with mosaics, acrylic paints, or polymer clay.

MOUNTING A BIRDHOUSE

Birds like their homes to feel safe and secure. Many prefer a house mounted on a vertical surface, such as a tree, fence post, or wall. A house placed on a tree or post near a wooded area makes a cozy spot for cavity-nesting birds such as chickadees, titmice, and nuthatches. Mounting the house on a metal garden post makes siting easy, but do follow the siting specifications for the given type of house (see the chart on page 79).

While hanging doesn't offer the stability of a stationary mount, it works well for designs such as hollowed-out gourds, which make great homes for a variety of birds, including house wrens, purple martins, and blue-birds. If you plan to hang your house from a tree, make sure you choose a branch that will provide solid support. To prevent damage to the branch, pad it with fabric or inner-tube rubber where you plan to attach the wire.

Posts vary in style and durability; they can be metal or wooden, and square or round. If you prefer wood, always use either pressure-treated lumber or a rot-resistant wood such as cedar. When mounting a house onto a tree trunk, first attach the house to a batten (a board about twice the height of the house) and then attach the batten to the tree. Do keep in mind that hardware can harm smaller trees. Some "tree-friendly" alternatives include fitting a wire around the trunk and attaching the house securely to the wire, or simply nailing a wooden crosspiece to the back of the house

A conical metal barrier (or baffle) attached to a post or pole will block squirrels and raccoons from climbing up to the birds' front door. Baffles can be constructed to fit both round and square posts, and should be installed at least five feet above ground level. If you have a hanging birdhouse, be sure to use heavy wire instead of rope; it's harder to climb. For added protection, metal pie pans make great homemade baffles and are easy to install on the wire.

Placing a metal guard around the entrance hole keeps squirrels from chewing their way inside. For protection against raccoons, try framing the entrance with a one-inch-thick block of wood. (Simply drill a hole the same size as the entrance opening through the block of wood and attach it over the entrance opening.) Spreading chicken wire just above the ground beneath the birdhouse considerably compromises a cat's ability to carry out a surprise attack. Bear in mind, however, that one of the most effective ways to deter intruders is to follow closely the recommendations for proper dimensions and siting for your birdhouse.

Unfortunately, birdhouses also make attractive home sites for nest-building insects such as wasps and bees. Don't despair. Coating the inside of the house with bar soap or Vaseline can discourage these tiny nesters. If you use an insect spray instead, be sure to choose one that is safe for birds.

and situating it firmly among several branches. Just be sure to balance your efforts to protect the trees with wise measures to deter predators.

DETERRING UNWANTED GUESTS
Along with nurturing and protecting feathered friends with food and shelter comes the responsibility for keeping competitors and predators at bay. Sparrows and starlings are the most aggressive competitors. They'll nest almost anywhere, and they begin building their homes earlier in the season than most birds (usually in late winter). The good news is that their nests can usually be cleaned out before your intended tenants arrive to claim their new home. Another way to discourage sparrows and starlings is to purchase or make a house with a slotted entrance opening rather than a round hole, or simply plug the entrance hole during the winter months. (Remember to unplug the hole in early spring when other birds are ready to begin nesting.)

As nature would have it, eggs and nestlings are vulnerable to the appetites of predators such as cats, raccoons, snakes, and squirrels. Your birds will enjoy a more peaceful home life if you install protective barriers that prevent uninvited guests from visiting them.

CLEANING

Birds don't enjoy coming home to a messy house any more than you do. You'll need to clean out the birdhouse after each nesting and again in early spring. Beware of wasps, and protect your hands with gloves. First remove and discard old nesting materials (a kitchen spatula or paint scraper works well), along with any uninvited ten-ants such as mice or insects. Then clean the inside of the house with a stiff brush and soapy water. Be sure to rinse thoroughly. Ridding the house of pests and parasites will make it fresh and inviting for the next family. Your newfound friends will appreciate your kind attention to their homes, and the reward will be yours when they return the following year.

Birdhouse Specifications

SPECIES	FLOOR (INCHES)	INTERIOR HEIGHT (INCHES)	ENTRANCE DIAMETER (INCHES)	ENTRANCE ABOVE FLOOR (INCHES)	HEIGHT ABOVE GROUND (FEET)
American Kestrel	8 x 8	12–15	3	9–12	10–30
Ash-Throated Flycatcher	6 x 6	8–10	$1\frac{1}{2}$	6–8	8–20
Barn Owl	10 x 8	15–18	6	0–4	12–18
Bewick's Wren	4 x 4	6–8	$1\frac{1}{4}$	4–6	5–10
Bluebird (Eastern, Mountain, Western)	4 x 4	8–12	$1\frac{1}{2}$	6–10	3–6
Carolina Wren	4 x 4	6–8	$1\frac{1}{2}$	4–6	5–10
Chickadee	4 x 4	9	$1\frac{1}{8}$	7	4–15
Downy Woodpecker	4 x 4	9	$1\frac{1}{4}$	7	5–15
Finch (House, Purple)	5 x 5	6	2	5–7	8–12
Flicker	7 x 7	16–18	$2\frac{1}{2}$	14–16	6–30
Great Crested Flycatcher	6 x 6	8–10	$1\frac{3}{4}$	6–8	8–20
Hairy Woodpecker	6 x 6	12–15	$1\frac{5}{8}$	9–12	12–20
House Wren	4 x 4	6–8	1–$1\frac{1}{4}$	4–6	4–10
Nuthatch	4 x 4	9	$1\frac{3}{8}$	7	5–15
Purple Martin	6 x 6	6	$2\frac{1}{4}$	1	10–20
Red-Headed Woodpecker	6 x 6	12	2	9	10–20
Robin	6 x 8	8	2	2	6–15
Screech Owl	8 x 8	12–15	3	9–12	10–30
Titmouse	4 x 4	9	$1\frac{1}{4}$	7	5–15
Wood Duck	12 x 12	22	4	17	10–20

Bluebird House

To foil the English sparrows and starlings that have displaced bluebirds in so many of their natural habitats, this easy-to-make bluebird house has a special, slotted entryway—one which helps prevent invasions from unwanted visitors. You may either build the house with a rot-resistant wood such as cedar and leave it unfinished, or use a standard softwood such as pine and apply an exterior finish.

MATERIALS & TOOLS

- Measuring tape
- Pencil
- Straightedge
- Circular saw or handsaw
- Table saw or ripsaw
- Clamps
- No. 2 Phillips-head screwdriver
- Electric drill with 1/8" bit
- Sandpaper
- No. 6 decking screws, 1 1/4"
- 3/32 x 1 3/8" screw hook

TIPS

- You'll need a 4'-long 1 x 6, and a 6 1/2"-long piece of 1 x 8 to make this project. As you shop for this lumber, remember that a 1 x 6 is 3/4" thick and 5 1/2" wide, and a 1 x 8 is 3/4" thick and 7 1/2" wide.
- The sides (A), floor (B), door (C), and roof (E) are ripped (cut to make them narrower) from 1 x 6 and 1 x 8 lumber. The easiest way to rip boards is with a table saw, but if you don't own one, you can use a handheld ripsaw. Be sure to clamp the boards securely before ripping.

CUTTING LIST

CODE	DESCRIPTION	QTY.	MATERIAL
A	Sides	2	3/4" x 4 3/4" x 9 1/2"
B	Floor	1	3/4" x 4" x 4"
C	Door	1	3/4" x 4" x 7 3/4"
D	Back	1	1 x 6 x 12"
E	Roof	1	3/4" x 6 1/2" x 6 1/2"

Instructions

1 From the 1 x 6, measure and cut the following lengths: 17 3/4", 4", and 7 3/4". Then rip the 17 3/4" piece to 4 3/4" in width, and the 4" and 7 3/4" pieces to 4" in width. Rip the 6 1/2"-long 1 x 8 to 6 3/4" in width. If you have access to a table saw, bevel cut one end of this 6 1/2" x 6 1/2" board to 17 degrees. (Don't worry if you can't make this cut.)

2 To cut the two sides (A), first set the 17¾"-long piece flat on your work surface, positioning it vertically. Then measure down 9½" from the upper left-hand corner and mark the long edge at this point. Next, measure up from the bottom right-hand corner, and mark the other long edge at 9½".

3 Join the two 9½" marks by drawing a diagonal line across the face of the board. Then cut along this marked line to create the two sides (A).

4 Place the two sides (A) flat on your work surface, with their short edges facing each other and their long edges facing outward. On each side, mark two pilot-hole positions: one ⅜" up from the short bottom end and 2" in from the longest side, and another 5¼" up from the short bottom end and ⅜" in from the short edge. Using an electric drill and ⅛" bit, predrill pilot holes at these marks.

5 To provide for drainage through the 4" x 4" floor (B), cut off the tip of each corner of this piece. Remove only a small amount of wood as you make these cuts.

6 To fasten the floor (B) to one side (A), position the side on its long edge, and place an edge of the floor against it so that the bottom face of the floor is flush with the bottom end of the side. Insert a 1¼" screw through

the pilot hole to fasten the parts together. Repeat to fasten the other side to the opposite edge of the floor.

7 Fit the 4" x 7¾" door (C) between the sides (A); its outer face should be flush with the sides' front edges and its top end should be 1⅛" below the top front corners of the sides. Fasten the door in place with a 1¼" screw inserted through the pilot hole in each side. Then back the two screws out slightly so the door will swing freely outward from the bottom.

8 Position the box with the door (C) face down. Place the back (D) on top of the sides (A) so that its bottom end hangs over the bottom ends of the sides by 1". Predrill four pilot holes through the back, placing each hole 4" from an end of the back and ⅜" in from a long edge. Then drive four 1¼" screws into the pilot holes.

9 Drill two ⅛" holes in the back (D) for mounting the birdhouse, each ½" in from an end and centered across the back's width.

10 Drill four pilot holes through the 6½"-square roof (E): two holes each ⅞" in from an edge and 1½" down from the bevel-cut end; and two holes, each ⅞" in from an edge and 4½" from the bevel cut end. (If you didn't bevel cut the roof, you may take these measurements from either end.)

11 Center the roof (E) on top of the angle-cut ends of the sides (A), with a ½" overlap at each edge, and the bevel-cut end of the roof pressed against the front face of the back (D). Secure the roof in place with four 1¼" screws.

12 Insert the screw hook into the front edge of one side (A), ⅝" from the side's bottom end. To prevent the door (C) from opening, turn the screw hook to a horizontal position. When it's time to clean out the birdhouse, turn the screw hook up or down, and pull the bottom edge of the door upward and outward.

Skyward Growth

Often when we hear the word *garden*, we think of our own earthbound beds teeming with color and life. Rarely do we regard the sky as a potential canvas for bright leaves and petals, fragrant blooms, or even tasty edibles. But skyward growth —anxious vines rambling atop high fences, arching arbors, and towering trellises—works wonders for a flat, uninteresting landscape. Use the techniques and ideas in these pages to prompt and train vines up, up, up . . . and create an exciting vertical dimension in your yard.

TRELLISES

The simplest way for you to add skyward growth to your garden is to use a trellis (a flat, latticework screen). The gridlike design of the trellis creates a ladder that makes it easier for vines to scramble their way upward. You'll find trellises made of any number of sturdy, rot-resistant materials, but wood and metal are the most popular choices. Some designs are purely functional and encourage maximum growth, showing your plantings to their best advantage. Others are more ornamental and offer a simple way to dress up

your garden—though you'll want nothing so flashy as to steal the show your clematis provides.

Readily available at your local home and garden center, trellises are so easy to build that you might want to consider making your own. To do so, first sketch out a trellis design. Use one of the patterns illustrated in these pages, or render one from your own imaginings. Now, choose your wood. Cedar, black locust, and white oak all fare well in the face of the elements with no stain or finish work required. On the other hand, softwoods such as pine are considerably less expensive

and will work perfectly well for a seasonal trellis that you store away in winter. Another, more rustic option for a seasonal trellis is to scavenge branches and saplings, as shown in the Birdbath Trellis project on page 84.

Start with 1 x 2s for the vertical pieces of the trellis; use thicker, stronger wood for the horizontals. If you've integrated curves into your design, use a jigsaw to cut them from plywood, or (if your budget allows) use extension jambs for arched windows. Cut the wood using a backsaw, which features fine teeth and leaves a more refined edge than a handsaw. If you've chosen a softwood, give it a layer of outdoor latex before assembling. Attach the individual pieces with screws, which will hold better than nails, being sure to drill pilot holes first to prevent the wood from splitting. Avoid rusty hardware by using galvanized screws only. Now, hang or stake your creation, plant, and watch as lush greenery reaches for the sky!

OTHER TREILLAGE

Besides the basic trellis, a number of other structures can display skyward growth. An arbor is like a long trellis that bends overhead to form an arch. (Alternatively, the arbor may be squared off at the top or consist of an overhead trellis supported by posts.) The arbor may serve as a garden entryway, or it may shade a quiet bench with a tangle of roses. If the arbor is especially sturdy, hang a swing from up top and enjoy

the fragrance of the blooms as you sail through the breeze. If an arbor is large enough, it will qualify as a pergola, which provides not only backyard romance but summertime shade. (Find more information on pergolas on page 43.) Arbors and pergolas both may seem like a lot of area to plant and maintain. However, after a few seasons of caring for basic trellis plantings, you should have no trouble coaxing these looming structures to life.

Great Climbing Plants

- **Wisteria** (*Wisteria*)
- **Jasmine** (*Jasminum*)
- **Morning Glory** (*Ipomoea*)
- **Scarlet Honeysuckle**
  (*Lonicera sempervirens*)
- **Black-eyed Susan vine**
  (*Thurnbergia alata*)

Sundial

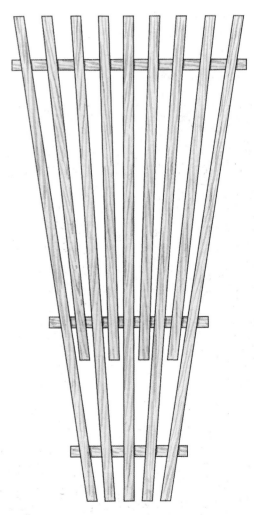

Japanese fan

Towering Birdbath Trellis

A birdbath trellis is a simple way to transform your birdbath into a handsome garden accent or centerpiece. When the trellis is covered with the bright blooms or edible fruit of the plants listed on the opposite page, you'll have created a colorful attraction for birds and butterflies.

MATERIALS & TOOLS

- 13 branches, 7' to 9' in length
- 6 crosspieces, 3' to 4' in length
- Handsaw
- Nails
- Hammer
- Twine

TIP

- Use branches leftover from tree prunings or gathered from a storm cleanup. Willow, bamboo, and any saplings all work well.

Instructions

1 First, cut the branches to size. The rustic character of this trellis allows for some flexibility in length; the more varied, the more natural appeal it maintains.

2 Lay out three separate V-shaped arrangements of branches, grouping four branches in each of the outer arrangements and five branches in the middle one. Be sure to lay the branches so that their stouter ends are at the bottom.

3 Measure and mark two points from the bottom of one of the branches, one at 6" and the other at 18". Repeat this step for the remainder of the branches.

4 Gather the crosspieces. Align the marked points of each of the four branches in the first arrangement, and place a crosspiece at each row of marked points. Use a hammer and nails to attach the crosspieces to the branches. Repeat this for the other two arrangements thereby forming three individual, grid-like sections of the trellis.

5 Now, dig a 6"- to 8"-deep trench in the shape of a half-circle around the back side of the birdbath.

6 Sink the individual sections into the trench until secure and tamp dirt around the base of each. Adjust the sections as needed to create a cave-like effect around the birdbath.

7 Use twine to join the edges of the left-hand section and the center section, weaving in and out of the branches and their crosspieces. Secure the right-hand section to the assembly in the same fashion. This will allow the vines to crawl over all three sections.

8 Plant the trellis with one of the fruit-bearing vines listed to the right, and watch as the birds flock to the abundance of fresh edibles.

FRUIT-BEARING CLIMBERS

Passiflora

Several vines in particular are eager to climb your trellis and attract birds. Just be sure to choose a plant that will thrive in your area without becoming invasive; an expert at your local nursery should be able to provide this information.

- Everyone loves the sweet, tart flavor of **kiwi fruit** (*Actinidia deliciosa*)—including birds. Plant the kiwi vine in fertile, well-drained soil and keep it sheltered from the wind. For optimal fruiting, give it full sun and prune it in late winter.

- The woody, deciduous **porcelain vine** (*Ampelopsis brevipedunticula*) climbs quickly, thanks to the fine tendrils that spiral out from its branches. Keep an eye out for pests, though; Japanese beetles will sometimes consume the berries before the birds are fed.

- A variety of species of **passionflower** (*Passiflora*, above) bloom and grow across the globe. Their exquisite flowers and small yellow fruit attract a variety of birds; those that flock to your yard will depend on your location.

- When we think of **potatoes** (*Solanum*) we usually envision deep-growing tubers rather than high-reaching vines. But the same plant that provides a hearty meal for humans has a cousin that feeds the birds. First, though, there will be a feast for your eyes, as the vines bear colorful spring and summer blooms.

GARDEN ART AND WHIMSY

Right: Is it a giant strand of DNA or a child's imagined ladder to the stars? Lyman Whitaker creates kinetic sculptures that spin and twirl at the whim of the winds. Using primarily bronze, Whitaker also sculpts backyard fountains and jewelry from his studio in the windy Utah desert.

Left: When gophers launched their attack on San Francisco's Garden for the Environment, Brooke Gelber fought back by fashioning this fun and functional pinwheel. Made entirely from scrap metal, the wind toy is loosely assembled so that when the wind blows, the rattling nuts and bolts send an annoying hum along the deeply buried metal pole. While the sound is nearly inaudible to the human ear, the pillaging rodents down below hear the message loud and clear—scram!

Left: Skyward growth, indeed! Nature itself is capable of many a feat, but this time around, arborist Richard Reames of Oregon's Arborsmith Studios had some input. Reames painstakingly trained this hybrid poplar tree into a form he's dubbed "The Spiral of Life." Inspired by the famed 1950's spectacle of Axel Erlandson's Tree Circus, Reames has shaped hundreds of trees in his bizarre and wonderful career.

Right: Since 1985, North Carolinian Vollis Simpson has been farming. It's not cotton or soybeans you'll find in his fields, but rather, massive whirligigs planted row on row. The seeds of Simpson's unique crop? Everyday objects such as ice cream scoops, stop signs, bicycle tires, and soda cans. While the creation shown here was sized for use on a porch or patio, Simpson's pastures host homegrown contraptions that loom as high as forty feet.

earth

Kneel down and rake a gloveless hand through the soil. What is the earth like in your yard? Is it hard, red, and clayey? Still dusty from last season's drought? Or is it rich, moist, and ready for planting? No matter what kind of earth your backyard is blessed or cursed with, this chapter will show you how to make the most of it.

Learn to shape the earth to develop the landscape you've always wanted. Build a gently sloping berm to make a private nook that your neighbors will never know about; transform a ravine by adding terraces of lush plantings; or salvage barren soil with raised beds. Don't forget to send a pathway meandering through it all—but will it be brick, stone, or gravel? For true outdoor style, accent the pathway with colorful mosaic stepping stones that you make by hand (we'll show you how!).

Finally, survey the tools and equipment you'll need to make it all happen. These pages will show you the weekend gardener's collection of spades, forks, and secateurs. Also, find great tips for storage and maintenance, including step-by-step instructions for making your own tool tote!

Paths and Walkways

It's easy to focus so intently on the separate plots and patches you've planted in your yard that you lose sight of the overall design. In addition to serving a practical purpose by connecting point A to point B, a path is the perfect way to create visual coherence by drawing together individual garden components.

DESIGN CONSIDERATIONS

No matter where your path will lead, plan its design before you start the work. Outlining specific design strategies now will save labor down the road. Will your path lead to or run beside a building? If so, it must slope away from the structure, either along its length or across its width, to prevent water damage. Will the roots of trees or other large plants extend beneath the path? Then choose a material (such as concrete) that will withstand such pressure. Consider the climate of your area, as well. In areas prone to heavy rainfall, you'll want a reliable drainage system beneath your path, or it may become a rushing stream! And if your region experiences frequent ground freezes or other temperature extremes, prepare a base that's especially deep and wide.

You don't have to be an expert to devise a good layout; you know your backyard better than anyone. Experimenting on paper is infinitely easier than hauling around piles of stone, so start by making some sketches, taking the shapes and lines of your outdoor space into account. Are they sharp and angular? Then a gentle, curving path will provide contrast and balance. Study your home and any existing structures in your backyard, too. Since these elements will share a space with the pathway, you may want to repeat their shapes and lines in your plan.

GETTING STARTED

When you've done some brainstorming on paper, try "sketching" on a larger scale. Use several lengths of rope or garden hose to outline the path's design; then stake pin flags (available at home improvement centers) along the way. When you are satisfied with the layout, remove the hose and use a brightly colored spray paint to mark the area of excavation. This may seem like overzealous planning but it will prevent labor-intensive damage control later.

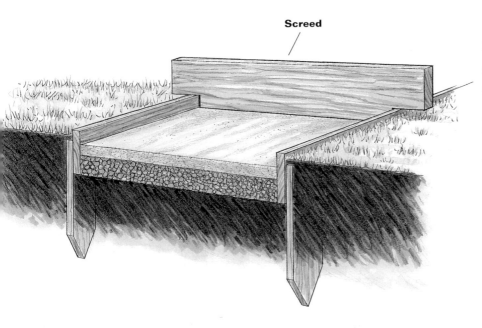

Screed

Before you begin digging, gather some tools and materials that will ease your task:

■ You will need a string level to grade the site and also to lay an even bed of finishing materials.

■ A screed is a board that you rake across the top of grading materials to ensure even distribution. Make your own screed by notching the ends of a wooden board, as shown in the illustration above.

■ An iron rake will allow you to spread gravel and mulch with ease.

■ Use a measuring tape to establish uniform width along the pathway.

■ Your digging and finishing tools will vary according to the material that you use but may include a spade (for cutting sod), a mallet (to tamp stones into place) and/or a trowel set (for spreading mortar).

LAYING A BASE

Pathways made with bricks, stones, concrete, and other heavy paving materials should rest on a base that will ensure good drainage and prevent frost heaving. To create a standard base, first dig a trench that's a uniform depth of six inches and a width that meets the predesignated edges of the intended pathway. Spread three inches of washed gravel—called "crusher run"—in the bottom of the trench, using your screed to level. Next, layer a precut piece of landscape cloth over the gravel in order to inhibit weed growth. At this point, you may wish to place edging material along the sides of the trench. Depending on the function of the path, this may consist of bricks, pressure-treated 2 x 4s, or decorative material such as the iron scrollwork lining the moss path below.

Finally, finish the base by spreading an inch of sand over the landscape cloth. (If you are building a brick path, fill the remaining three inches with sand. This creates a ground-level path with superior drainage.) You are now ready to pave.

This base works for most paths, but there are a few exceptions. Grass paths, for example, just need a three-inch-deep trench and no sand or crusher run. Stepping stones require that you excavate only around the edges of the individual stones. Note too that in areas where drainage is exceptionally poor, the base should be deeper and V-shaped. A drainage pipe set on one inch of gravel in the trench's bottom helps carry away water.

Paving Possibilities

Before you start building a path, you'll want to carefully consider which material is best for your backyard. Your options are many, and even if you have a clear idea of what you'd like, taking the time to think through the practical implications of your choice will let you feel more confident in your undertaking.

First, assess the site of your future walkway. Is it dry or damp? Steep or level? Heavily trafficked or a quiet nook? The answers to these questions will all be factors in your choice of paving material. Also, ask yourself how much time and effort you'd like to invest in this project as well as your level of skill and experience with various materials. Do you feel qualified to lay the path yourself, or should you hire an expert to do the work? Some materials are easier to work with than you think, and you may be surprised at your own capabilities. For instance, most weekend gardeners can expect to lay a gravel path in a long day or a short weekend.

Next, consider the availabilty and expense of different materials. Your local home improvement center will host a wide and varied selection of paving materials. However, native or

Mulch

locally manufactured materials are often less expensive when purchased directly from the source, and they will likely be more appropriate for your terrain. For example, a quarry or stone yard might be the best place to buy gravel or cut stone. You're bound to find a bargain on wood chips at a saw mill, so take advantage if there's one nearby. Also, keep your eyes peeled for local demolition sites, where you could reap enough brick or stone to pave several paths.

Before the vast range of possibilities overwhelms you, consult the following quick and easy reference. These pages will guide you through the advantages, disadvantages, cost, and maintenance of the most popular paving materials.

MULCH

Speading mulch is quite possibly the easiest way to lay a path. If the drainage of your chosen site is already good, then you won't even need to dig a base. Instead, scrape away the top

layer of growth, lay a pre-sized piece of landscape cloth, and rake three inches of mulch over the area. In addition to being light-weight and budget-friendly, mulch also requires minimal maintenance. In most cases, you'll only need to replenish path material yearly.

Of course, mulch is not the best choice for every backyard path. Before you snap this book shut and rush off to load your pickup with pine bales or bags of bark, think twice. In particularly soggy regions, frequent, heavy rain will lay waste to your labor in no time (especially on ungraded, sloping sites). Also, a mulch path that winds through unkempt growth will inevitably face weed invasion. Meanwhile, a dry, well-tended site will welcome the addition of a mulch walkway. Whether you opt for pine needles, bark, or wood chips, mulch will add a spring to your step and give your path a comfortable, informal feel.

MOSS AND GRASS

Though we usually envision a walkway winding through the green, a unique and lush alternative is to create a path that is itself green. Both grass and moss are inexpensive paving options for backyard walkways;

though neither is quite as easy to work with as the aforementioned mulch. In sunny, moderate climates, grass will fare well and enhance the surrounding beds of bright blooms. To create a grass path, transfer sod (available at both garden centers and sod farms) rather than sowing grass seed. Laying sod is hard work but it will yield cleaner lines and quicker results than just spreading seed over the site.

To minimize maintenance and maximize effect, do some research to make sure the grass you use is one that will suit your purposes. Will the path be heavily trafficked? Bermuda, cen-

tipede, or zoysia stand up to excessive use but tend to fade during the colder seasons. Meanwhile, under the right circumstances, evergreen grasses such as fescue, bluegrass, and rye will thrive year-round. If you are unsure which type of grass is best for your walkway, consult a lawn care manual.

Too much rain could turn a fledgling course of grass into a mudslide, but still, a carpet of green can be yours. For damp, shady areas, moss provides an excellent alternative to the grass path—and adds unmatched sensuality to your garden. A moss path takes time; you'll probably have to collect and transfer it bit by bit. Jump-start this process by using a blender to mix the moss with a bit of milk. Spread the mixture over the site, then keep the area moist to accelerate spore reproduction. When your path is ready, kick off your shoes—there's nothing like bare feet against a cool, moss path.

BRICK

The stately appeal of brick starkly contrasts with the casual ease of mulch, grass, and moss. The small size of these baked clay pavers (shown in the photo

Brick

above) makes for both versatility and simplicity in the laying process. Most often found in standard maroon, brighter red, or paler tan, brick is easily cut and shaped with a brick chisel. A brick path can be both practical and long-lasting, but requires that you pay close attention to the details:

■ Solid paving bricks withstand traffic better than semi-hollow facing bricks, which are intended for walls.

■ Significant root growth will quickly undermine your brick path by exerting upward pressure and causing the surface to buckle. Prevent such sabotage by siting your brick path away from large shrubs and trees.

■ When laying the base of your brick path, keep a close eye on the level throughout each stage of construction —otherwise, you'll end up with a rippling effect. Also add a few extra inches of sand above the landscape cloth; the elevation will improve drainage and extend the life of your path.

CONCRETE

Take advantage of this versatile and inexpensive material to create a path that's just right for your needs. If the path that you're imagining is purely functional (maybe you'd like to roll your wheelbarrow from your garden to your shed with ease), concrete offers the most straightforward solution available. And while you may not always associate concrete with creativity, in truth wet cement offers plenty of room for "play." You might pour a fresh batch of cement into molds—either preformed or handmade—to make your own unique paving stones. Or, manipulate the surface texture by using a broom, rake, or other tools (including your hands and feet!) to create fun patterns and designs. For a little pizazz in the backyard, embed stones, marbles, rhinestones, or found objects into the cement before it cures completely.

Before you get started, take into account that mixing and pouring cement is harder than it looks. While it's bound to remind you of making mud pies, rest assured that it is not quite as easy. Still, with a little practice, you can indeed pave your own concrete path. Do keep a guidebook handy, or if you're a true beginner, hire an expert to advise or assist you. For large jobs, you'll need a rented power cement mixer. When paving smaller areas, just mix by hand using a hoe and wheelbarrow. Other equipment you'll need includes expansion material to fill the joints between poured sections, a float (similar to a finishing trowel), and a tarp to protect the "curing" cement from inclement weather. Remember while you're working that

Quarried stone

concrete loses its durability if it's mixed too long—and you don't want to be faced with the task of pouring your pathway twice!

STONE

The effect that a stone path will have on your landscape depends largely on the way that the pavers are cut. The clean geometry of precut paving blocks (which may be rectangular, hexagonal, circular, or novelty-shaped) is often used to formalize outdoor settings. Meanwhile, natural fieldstone maintains a rustic and casual charm, especially when the cracks between stones are planted with aromatic thyme. For an aesthetic result that lands somewhere between these two extremes, choose the hard lines and

rugged textures of quarried stone. Types of stone that you might use in your backyard walkway include limestone (which acquires a weathered character over the years) and slate

(which holds up extremely well in the face of the elements). Though somewhat costly, exotic colored stone like rose or oak is also available.

To lay a stone path, construct a base as directed on page 91. Then begin paving. Laying stone is a bit like working a jigsaw puzzle; each piece will need to correspond to the confines of your path and to the surrounding pavers. (To help make each stone fit, you may want to use a circular saw with a masonry blade to shape and trim). When the pathway is complete, sweep sand over the top and into the cracks between stones. Spray with water and repeat this procedure until the sand is densely packed.

MOSAICS

If you're looking for a fun, inexpensive paving option, try mosaic. Mosaic is a process of surface decoration that involves inlaying small pieces of variously colored material, called **tesserae**, to form patterns and designs. Almost anything can serve as tesserae—and we do mean anything. Bottle caps, broken glass, marbles, terra cotta shards, and pebbles can all enhance your backyard with color and texture. You may embed these or other found objects into wet cement or adhere tesserae to storebought paving stones and then grout, as is demonstrated on page 96. The results can be smooth or textured, careful or crazed, colorful or subdued. Anything goes where mosaic is concerned, so first-timers, have no fear!

Colorful Mosaic Stepping Stones

Mosaic lends itself to the imagination in a way that no other medium does. While some care is required in cutting and setting the tiles, fledgling beginner and master mosaicist alike will enjoy this otherwise liberating process. Collecting the tiles will be half the fun: Orphan china plates, scrap bits from a tile distributor, or ceramic squares left over from your kitchen renovation all make excellent material for this project. Place finished stones in a pathway, as the photo below suggests, or position them in garden beds (as shown at right) to create convenient places to perch while you weed.

MATERIALS & TOOLS

- Pencil
- Paper, 12" x 18"
- Assorted tiles
- 3 or 4 lint-free rags
- Protective eye goggles
- Rubber mallet or hammer
- Tile nippers
- Premixed gray tile mastic, 1 pint
- Notched trowel
- Palette knife
- Dust mask
- Mixing container
- All-purpose powdered grout
- Several cups of water
- 12" x 12" concrete stepping stone
- Grout sealer, 1 pint

TIPS

- Certainly there is more than one way to shatter tile. While hurling it against the floor or wall may sound recklessly appealing, resist the urge and refer to our instructions for a safer and more effective method.
- Grout fills the crevices between the tiles in your piece and reinforces the cohesion that the mastic provides. Many types of grout are available, including premixed and sand-free varieties. The kind you'll use for this project contains silica sand, which can damage the lungs—so don't forget the dust mask!
- These materials and instructions will yield one stone, but make as many as you like—the process is addictive, and practice makes perfect.

Instructions

1 With your paper and pencil, map out a design for your mosaic, accounting for the colors and patterns of the tiles that you've chosen. Don't bother making an especially elaborate or detailed pattern, or you'll be frustrated when it's time to cut the tile.

2 Slip on your safety goggles and prepare to break the tile into bits (called tesserae). Do so one piece at a time by wrapping a tile in two layers of rag and, using the mallet or hammer, pounding steadily upon the wrapped tile until you're pleased with the shapes and sizes you've achieved.

3 Assemble the tesserae on your paper template, using the tile nippers to refine the shapes of the tiles as needed.

4 Spread mastic over the surface of the concrete stone, creating a uniform series of ridges with your trowel.

5 Begin transferring tesserae from the template to the stone, firmly embedding each piece in the mastic that you've spread. Allow the mastic to dry overnight.

6 Wearing your dust mask, begin mixing the powdered grout by following the instructions on the

Alternative Tesserae

For an impressively improvised effect, substitute any of the following materials for the tile bits used in this project:

- Pebbles, marbles, or stones
- Dominoes, dice, or checkers
- Polished glass or bits of mirror
- Wooden puzzle pieces
- Beads or sequins of varying shapes and sizes
- Bottle caps, buttons, or shells

package. You'll want the final product to have a consistency similar to cake icing. With the palette knife, spread the mixture over the mosaic, filling every nook and cranny. Let the grout set about 30 minutes, then use a damp rag to wipe away the excess.

7 When the grout has dried completely (allow at least 24 hours) apply a sealer to help protect the grout from harsh weather. Leave your finished project in a sheltered area to dry for two full days; then place it in the garden.

Patios

Nothing says backyard living like a well-used, well-tended patio. Most often constructed adjacent to the house, a patio typically serves as a transition area between the home and the great outdoors. Where else can you prepare a feast in the open air, or allow the songbirds to lull you to sleep, or drink in fresh breezes with your morning coffee? Here, find ideas and inspiration that will lure you out the back door and right into the peaceful splendor of your new patio.

PLANNING YOUR PATIO

Constructing a patio is much like building a great, wide path. So, if you've already laid a path in your backyard, then you should feel comfortable building a patio. Some special considerations do apply, though. For instance, the sheer size of a patio makes the cost more significant than that of the average pathway. (A patio may in fact be the single greatest expenditure that you make for the betterment of your outdoor space.)

Rather than being a means to a destination, a patio is a destination itself. The first thing that you'll need

to do is find the ideal site in your yard for a patio. Most likely this will be a place where you already spend a substantial amount of time; maybe the spot faces your glimmering koi pond, or maybe it's nestled beneath your favorite oak. While most patios are sited in close proximity to the house, you may choose otherwise. Remote locations can offer unmatched tranquility, so if you'd rather, position the patio behind some hedges or at the end of a winding pathway.

On the practical side, you'll want a location that's somewhat level and that features good drainage. If no such site exists in your yard, use fill dirt or transfer earth from other parts of your yard to modify the landscape.

To determine the size of your patio, ask yourself how many people will occupy the space at one time. Will it be used for solo sunbathing or for large family cookouts? In general, allot 32 square feet per person for the first three people, then 21 square feet for each additional person using the patio. Factor in the space occupied by any patio furniture, as well. This may include "kitchen" gear like a grill, utensil rack, and dining table; lounging furniture such as a hammock, chaise, or day bed; or children's play equipment such as a sandbox or wading pool.

With the intended square footage in mind, draw out some shapes that suit the layout of your yard. In doing so, take into account the paving material you'll use; it can be difficult, for instance, to achieve a strong curve with square-cut stones. Feel free to be

creative—angle the patio, rather than flushing it square against the house, or use hexagonal slabs to lay an irregularly shaped patio. Do think twice about especially outlandish designs, though—this will be a fairly permanent addition to your backyard. Finalize the plan by making a to-scale drawing of the patio.

EXECUTING YOUR DESIGN

Now, use a measuring tape to find the points in your landscape that correspond to your drawing and stake pin flags accordingly. You excavate the base of the patio in much the same way that you did the pathway (see page 90). It is vital, however, that you build well below the **damp-proof course** of the building. This means that the surface of the patio is six inches below the siding of your house. Often mandated by city building codes, this distance will protect the siding of the building from splashing rainwater. Excavating such depths may put your shovel dangerously close to utility lines, so know where yours lie before you begin. Also, due to the exceptional surface area of a patio, it is even more important that the paved area slope slightly away from any surrounding buildings. Before you pave the patio, you'll need to grade the site. Spread a layer of soil that thickens as it reaches the structure; start with at least three inches and work outward to about six. When you're finished, pour yourself a tall iced drink, kick back on the chaise, and find out what backyard living is all about.

Hedges and Topiary

Is clipping your hedges a tedious chore, or is it a creative outlet? Topiary—the practice of sculpting plants into ornaments—has weathered centuries of gardeners' whims. Derived from the Greek word *topos*, meaning landscape, *topiary* first referred to the trees, hills, and valleys artisans added to the walls of high-society homes by chiseling bas-relief or painting frescoes. This was a means of bringing the outdoors in.

Before long, *topiary* was used to describe a way of bringing the indoors out, as gardeners began creating intimate outdoor rooms walled by intricate hedgework. Ancient and medieval topiary masters studied for decades to perfect the art of clipping and coaxing plants into grandiose shapes and forms. That fact, however, need not intimidate you. Today, weekend gardeners armed with basic knowledge and the right tools can sculpt their own bright, textured marvels. Look through the topiary essentials that follow; then pick up your shears and let your imagination lead you!

SUPPLIES

The tools and materials that you'll need to gather for your topiary project will depend on the type of work that you are doing. For small topiaries and branches less than 3/4 inch, invest in a pair of double-blade bypass pruners, or opt for the more economical but shorter-lived single-blade anvil pruners. Long-handled loppers or hedge shears can cut branches less than two inches in diameter; for those as thick as four inches, a serrated Grecian handsaw will do the trick. Larger jobs—reno-

vating adult hedges, for example—call for a chain saw or a hefty handsaw.

Other helpful topiary gear includes sturdy, flexible wire to make frames and templates; string to guide your clippers along a straight line; and fishing line to hold moss in frames. You'll also need plastic sheeting to catch stray clippings and to simplify your cleanup. Pair these basic supplies with a little imagination, and you'll have no trouble sculpting your own living statuary!

PLANTS FOR TOPIARY

Boxwood, rosemary, and juniper—the first shrubs to be sculpted in topiary history—have remained popular with scissor-happy gardeners. The plants that you choose for your own back-yard will depend on the type of topiary project you wish to undertake.

When working with potted topiary, use herbs such as thyme or sage, or flowering shrubs like azalea or lilac. For hedges, your choices abound: Stalwart evergreens, broadleaf shrubs, and bountiful dwarf fruit trees all lend themselves to inventive or traditional sculpting.

For knot gardens, use shrubs, herbs, and flowers that mature at a low height. This will allow you to enjoy your design from an aerial perspective and to step easily over the border growth to weed and water the garden. Dwarf boxwood can provide the clean, classic lines of the knot, while pansies, violets, and lavender deliver contrasting color and texture.

If children will be frolicking afoot, then use plants that are nontoxic and free of thorns. Plants with ornamental or edible fruit, such as dwarf fruit trees, will attract birds, while fine-textured shrubs like barberry or yew provide visual variety. Each of these is available bare-root, container-grown, or balled-and-burlapped. No matter which plants you prefer, choose those with tall, upright growing habits, favorable leaf density, and color that complements any surrounding foliage.

POTTED TOPIARY

If you find the scale of traditional topiary intimidating, try a smaller, contained version of this living sculpture. Potted topiaries are perfect for porches

and decks and can be moved around the garden at your whim. (Before you get started, choose a container using our guide on page 112.)

Quick-growing vines—ivy and creeping fig, for example—are easily trained onto treillage or frames shaped like hearts, circles, and simple garden critters. To make your own, bend a length of sturdy, flexible wire into the desired shape. Use pliers to refine the shape if necessary. Be sure to leave a 12- to 15-inch stem on the end of the wire so that you can stake the shape into the potting soil, giving it a hair-pin curve to anchor it firmly. Twine the plant's shoots up around the shape, tying them in place if necessary.

Water and fertilize the plant regularly to encourage fast growth, and either prune new shoots that appear or add them in by also twining them onto the frame. If your topiary is a houseplant, you'll need to turn it regularly to keep the growth from becoming lopsided.

An even simpler topiary effect can be had by simply trimming the fine leaves of an herb into a textured mound; rosemary, thyme, and sage all work well for this style. Ivy and other climbing vines respond well to trellis-style prompting, and potted fruit trees actually produce more fruit when cut into shapes which expose more of the plants' surfaces to light.

PLANTING HEDGES

Following their debut in ancient Greece, shaped hedges cropped up again in England, where farmers used them to keep cattle from wandering astray. While your own herd is more likely to consist of pets and toddlers, hedges remain an invaluable garden feature in terms of both form and function. Their foliage creates a soft, colorful barrier that offers privacy from nearby neighbors, shelter from the wind, and organic architecture to the garden.

Plant your own hedge using the guide in these pages to help you find the tree or shrub that best suits your needs. Determine the number of plants that you'll need by measuring the length of the space that you'd like to plant, and then dividing by the dis-tance you'll need between each plant. This distance will always depend on size of the mature plant. Generally, though, you'll want to factor 36 to 60 inches between trees, while shrubs only need 18 to 30 inches.

Now, dig a trench that runs the length of your intended hedge—one that's deep and wide enough to accom-modate the root spread of your plants. Prune any damaged roots and bran-ches, then carefully place the plants in the trench. Add enough soil to fill the trench halfway. Soak the planting with water, and let it drain well before adding the remaining soil and water-ing again. Top the area with mulch (avoiding trunks or stems), and water the plants weekly for one to two grow-ing seasons.

KNOT GARDENS

Originally the brainchild of fifteenth-century Italian gardeners, the concept of the knot garden quickly spread to France and England. Though each country's approach differed from the next, the basic components of the knot garden included hedges, infill, and flowers in an intricate, aerially viewed arrangement of plants. The border was formed by a square (or otherwise geometric) hedge that completely sur-rounded the garden. The other hedges wound within this border. The name for these gardens comes from the the English tradition, where the inner hedge forms a continuous, unbroken knot. Infill such as gravel or sand is often used in the spaces between hedges to accentuate the knot design. Otherwise, you may plant flowers to add a perk of color to the landscape.

POPULAR TOPIARY SHAPES

A. The Spiral

B. The Archway

C. The Truncated Pyramid

D. The Ball-Shaped Standard

Raised Beds

This spring, transform that dusty span of hard-packed earth that passes as a backyard into a lush swath of color. Impossible? Not with the inventive advantage of raised beds. By constructing low retaining walls and filling them with rich, fertile soil, you can foster growth in your backyard in exciting new ways.

If the native soil in your garden is already superior, then you may still find reasons to construct raised beds. The elevated growing areas keep curious children and frisky pets from trampling plants. The height of a raised bed also offers convenience to elderly or physically impaired gardeners who may need to work from a seated position. Usually, a raised bed can both jump-start and extend the growing season by retaining solar heat and providing good drainage.

BUILDING A RAISED BED

First, find a site in your garden that invites the addition of a raised bed. Because the soil in raised beds warms up quickly, you might want to choose an area of partial shade. If you're planning on using the bed for crops, avoid long beds running east to west, since each plant will shade the next and stunt its growth.

A wide range of materials is avail-

able to create the retaining walls of your bed: dry-stacked stone, mortared brick, or cement, to name a few. (Railroad ties—formerly the most popular material for walls—are now known to contain chemicals hazardous to the health of the plants and to you, too.)

The most basic raised bed consists of three 2 x 4s, each measuring eight feet long. Cut one board in half to form the short sides of the bed. Stake the chosen site out with strings and pegs; then remove sod and large stones from that area. Till the soil in the bed area to a depth of several inches. Arrange the lumber in a rectangular shape around the edges of the bed, facing the widest part of the wood to the side. Use three-inch, rustproof screws to connect the ends of the lumber, and reinforce the frame with an L-bracket at each corner.

Now, use a carpenter's level to make sure that the frame sits evenly on the site. Add one part compost to nine parts professional soil mix to fill the bed. Water well, and fill with all of the plants you never thought would grow in your garden.

SPECIAL CONSIDERATIONS

What's great about raised beds is that they can be tailored in shape, form, and size to suit the needs of individual gardeners. If your garden is a hotspot for moles and gophers, for instance, head them off with chicken wire layered on the floor of the bed. If you'd

like to build a raised bed flush with the side of your home but worry about moisture collecting in the foundation wall or siding, just add a moisture-proof barrier to the back side of the planter. (A consultant at your local home improvement center can recommend the water-resistant material that will best protect your home.)

When building raised beds for physically challenged gardeners, leave enough space between beds to accommodate a wheelchair. Normally, a good 25 to 30 inches is enough to squeeze in a wheelbarrow, but a wheelchair needs 36 or 40 inches for safe passage. Also, build the beds high enough to allow access from a comfortably seated

position; generally this means no lower than 30 inches. Because the gardeners may prefer to sit on the edges of the bed, build retaining walls that are especially wide and sturdy. (You may follow the previous instructions for building a raised bed to achieve this effect, substituting 4 x 4s in place of 2 x 4s and stacking them several planks high.)

Berms

Despite your best efforts, it seems your backyard lacks a certain richness and comfort. No matter how many colorful perennials you add to your garden beds, you still aren't satisfied. You might dangle chimes from the tree branches, maybe add a few potted begonias to your patio, but something's not quite right. Before you hang up your gardening gloves for good, consider creating a berm. A berm is a mound, ledge, or wall of earth, guaranteed to revolutionize your outdoor space—and bring new meaning the phrase "earthmoving"!

WHY A BERM?

Constructing a berm will cure many a landscaping ailment. Often in suburbia each backyard seems to be a clone of the next. Most commonly this means flat, angular areas placed end on end for blocks and sectioned off with a length of chain-link fence. These outdoor spaces are difficult to personalize, and their squarish shapes can look severe and unnatural. These seemingly insurmountable issues are easily tackled when you begin to manipulate the terrain of your backyard. Bringing in a few piles of soil will alter the topography, whether drastically or subtly, and

your house or shed), then plan for your landscaping efforts to address that.

The earth that you use to create your berm can either be carved out of your existing landscape or brought in from a fill-dirt service. Either way, you'll probably want to hire a backhoe. Manual labor will certainly do the trick, but not without extraordinary expenditure of blood, sweat, and tears. Plan on acquiring enough soil to create a 4- to 5-foot-high mound. Unless constructed under the supervision of an expert, higher berms risk becoming mudslides.

Mix the soil with large, heavy rocks. This helps to define the area visually and prevents erosion, too. When the berm is in place, cover it with grass seed or thick mulch to stabilize the soil. After the grass has taken root or the mulch has settled somewhat, consider how you'd like to plant the berm: Tall ornamental grasses maximize privacy, while colorful flowers, foliage, and ground covers offer a visual treat.

make it unique. With good planning and a weekend or so of steady labor, the sharp lines and corners of your yard will soften, lending gentle curves and an enhanced dimension to the landscape. Strategically placed, a berm can offer your family just the seclusion it needs from the neighbor's barking dog or those loveable but rowdy kids next door.

The soft slope of a berm will also display plantings and garden statuary at an elevated height, making them even easier to admire. If your yard plays the unlucky host to eyesores like old well heads or steel pilings, consider veiling them behind an attractively-planted berm. This will eliminate the labor-intensive task of removing them.

Carefully considered, mounding soil in new ways may also alleviate drainage problems in your yard. The benefits of building a berm—and the ease with which it can be done—make many backyards likely candidates.

CREATING A BERM

Before you begin arbitrarily heaping dirt onto your lawn, determine what purpose you'd like your berm to serve. Will it be functional, decorative, or a little of each? If the drainage in your yard is good, consult a landscaper to ensure that it stays that way when you add the berm. If, on the other hand, drainage is a problem (symptoms include boggy soil, flash-flooding, erosion, and/or rot around the edges of

Terracing

Through the ages, people around the world have used terracing to transform steep slopes into land suitable for planting. Today, terraced gardens are built for decorative as well as practical purposes—to create nearly level areas for planting and to make slopes more attractive and accessible. Cutting a series of level plateaus into a slope also provides a perfect solution to drainage problems and adds visual variety to your overall landscape design.

VARYING YOUR PLANTING THEME

With careful planning, just about any kind of gardening is possible on a terraced slope. Trees provide pockets of shade for ferns, hostas, mosses, and hardy geraniums, while sunny spots offer perfect homes for bright perennials and annuals. Rock gardens brimming with phlox, sedum, purple sage, thyme, and other easy-care "creepers" add texture and variety to your garden theme. Terraces are also ideal settings for meandering trails and paths among seasonal flower beds and ground covers. An overall plan that is well suited to your site creates a stunning backdrop for a focal point such as a pond, bench, or stone wall.

Keep in mind that drought-tolerant plants grow well along steeper terraces, while "thirsty" plants thrive near the bottom. And remember that the most cherished garden evolves over time. Your terrace garden does not have to happen overnight. So relax and enjoy—one step at a time.

CHOOSING RETAINING WALLS

A terrace requires a retaining wall to hold back the soil in it. Desirable effects for terraced walls can be achieved with any number of creative combinations of building materials. Combining stacked stones with locust logs creates a warm, primitive look in a rustic backyard setting. Railroad ties and landscape timbers make good retaining-wall materials, as do slabs of recycled concrete walkway, and concrete blocks made to look like stone. Dry-stacked stone walls combined with dry-laid steps are not only practical but also provide decorative focal points that draw the eye.

SLOPING TERRACES TO ENHANCE DRAINAGE

Rather than making terraced levels flat, gently slope them from the center outward, allowing rainwater to run off to the sides. Avoid too much sloping, or heavy rain will wash away topsoil from beds and mulch from pathways. If your terraces include pathways, consider digging the paths six to nine inches below the level of planting beds, so that water will drain slowly along the path rather than pooling on the terraced bed.

PREPARATIONS

First you'll need to calculate the **rise** and **run** of your slope. Set a vertical stake at the top of the slope and another at the bottom. Tie a string between them, with a line level on it to make sure the string is level. Measure the longer stake from the string to the ground; this distance is the rise. The length of the string is the run. Divide the run by the desired number of terraces to determine the width of each terrace. Then divide the rise by the desired number of terraces to calculate the height of each terrace.

Also check the condition of the soil before deciding what to plant. Dig several test holes, and if you encounter many rocks, consider building a raised bed or planting a ground cover around the rocks. If you don't mind doing a little excavating, larger rocks can be dug out and used for building a dry-stacked wall.

To transform a large hillside or embankment, you'll probably need more than a shovel and your own two hands to do the job—consult a landscape professional. But for mild to moderate slopes that can be conquered "by hand," a dry-stacked stone wall can turn a sloped area into a productive and beautiful garden.

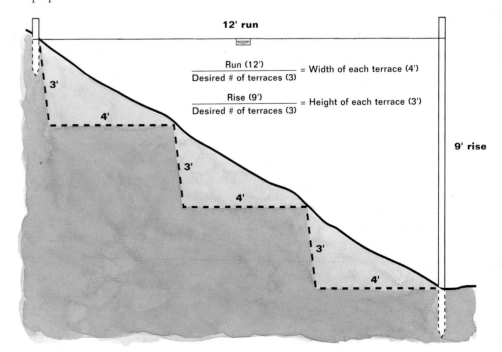

12' run

$$\frac{\text{Run (12')}}{\text{Desired \# of terraces (3)}} = \text{Width of each terrace (4')}$$

$$\frac{\text{Rise (9')}}{\text{Desired \# of terraces (3)}} = \text{Height of each terrace (3')}$$

3'

4'

3'

4'

3'

4'

9' rise

Portable Kneeling Pad

- For lack of pipe cutters, you may use a hacksaw to create the spacers as described in step 6. Pipe cutters, however, will make quicker and cleaner cuts.

- If the lettering on the side of the PVC becomes an eyesore, remove it by sanding it lightly.

- The rope shown in this project is classic jute, which looks great and will hold up well. Polypropylene cord may last even longer, though, and is available in splashy colors to satisfy your stylistic whims.

Instructions

1 Start by ripping the 2 x 4 cedar in half to make two pieces. This operation is best performed with a table saw. If you don't have one ask your local home improvement center to do the job for you (the fee for this is minimal).

2 Take one of the cedar strips and measure and mark 22" from one end. Place the wood in a vise and use your handsaw to make a clean, straight cut; this will yield your first slat. Continue measuring and sawing until you have cut four slats, then repeat with the second cedar strip.

S ay goodbye to filthy, gravel-embedded gardener's knees forever. Modeled after traditional beet paths that Polish farmworkers would carry with them to unroll in the fields, this convenient kneeling pad will save you hours of discomfort—not to mention gallons of laundry detergent! The cedar will resist rot for years so requires no sealant or other finish. If dressing it up with a colorful paint job makes weeding a friendlier task, though, be sure to find an appropriate outdoor latex for the job.

MATERIALS & TOOLS

- 2 x 4 cedar, 8' long
- Table saw
- Tape measure
- Pencil
- Handsaw

- Vise
- Electric drill and ⅜" bit (brad-point is best)
- Scrap wood
- Sanding block
- 150-grit sandpaper

- ½" PVC pipe, 8" long
- Pipe cutters
- ¼" rope, 7' long
- Masking tape
- ¾" poultry staples
- Hammer

CUTTING LIST

CODE	DESCRIPTION	QTY.	MATERIAL
A	Wooden Slats	8	1½" x 1½" x 22"
B	PVC Spacers	14	½"-long

3 Lay one slat across your work surface, measure 4" from each end, and mark a straight line at each point. Bisect each line by finding the center of the slat; this creates two intersections at which you'll drill in step 4. Repeat this step for each of the remaining slats.

4 Now you are ready to drill. Place a piece of scrap wood beneath the slat to catch the spinning bit and prevent splintering. With your drill and ⅜" bit, bore a hole straight through the two cross-marks on each of the eight slats.

5 With your sanding block and sandpaper, smooth the edges of each slat. When no sharp edges or splinters remain, set the slats aside.

6 Secure your PVC pipe in the vise and mark a line ½" from one end.

Use pipe cutters to make an even cut at the line, severing your first spacer from the pipe. Continue in this fashion until you have cut thirteen more spacers.

7 Prepare to thread the slats together: Lay them out on a table with the holes aligned and facing each other, so that the long dimension runs left to right. Wrap both ends of your rope in masking tape to prevent them from fraying while you work.

8 Push the wrapped end of the rope through the left-hand hole in the slat closest to you. When the rope comes through the other side of the slat, slip a spacer on the end and thread it through the prealigned hole in the next slat.

9 Continue until all of the slats are threaded and spaced along the left side. When you pull the rope through

the final hole, leave a "tail" that's long enough to reach the holes on the right of the assembly.

10 Hold the end of the rope you've just threaded against the side of the last slat approximately ½" to the right of the threaded holes. Attach it to the wood with a staple.

11 Begin threading the holes on the right-hand side of the assembly. Use the same method described in steps 8 and 9, remembering to add a spacer between each slat and to leave enough enough excess rope to reach the holes on the left side.

12 Give the rope an extra tug to pull out the slack—the spacers and slats should fit snugly but not tightly together—and secure the rope with a staple about ½" to the left of the newly threaded holes.

13 Now take the two ends of the rope and tie them together to form a handle for carrying the kneeling pad. Almost any knot will do, but the double fisherman's knot shown here holds well and looks great, too.

Double fisherman's knot

Container Gardening

Who can forget the sense of childlike wonder that came from planting seeds in a coffee can and waiting not so patiently for the first signs of green to poke through the soil? Container gardening takes us back to childhood —to the joys of planting, nurturing, and watching things grow.

Whether you're challenged by limited space or longing to enhance your existing garden, container plants can bring color, texture, dimension, and charm to any garden sanctuary. And one of the joys of container gardening is that you're not bound by any hard and fast rules. Let your whims lead the way.

CHOOSING CONTAINERS

A vast array of pots, bowls, troughs, barrels, urns, and tubs awaits you at your local home or garden center. As you shop for containers, consider those most suitable for your setting. If you'd rather indulge in a treasure hunt for "found" containers, try browsing at flea markets and antique stores or cleaning out the garage. Old boots, rustic baskets, your grandmother's wash basin, or an antique urn can all be turned into creative containers for plants.

As a general rule, natural materials make the best homes for plants— wood, stone, terra-cotta, and copper. The subtle earthiness of terra-cotta blends naturally with most plants, and these pots come in virtually every shape and size. Ceramic and terra-cotta pots, however, are vulnerable to freezing and cracking during harsh winters. Synthetic imitations are usually less costly, offer comparable visual appeal, and can withstand seasonal variations in temperature. Reconstituted stone and fiberglass containers also make good alternatives.

In terms of size, remember that large pots lend themselves to lush, dramatic displays. Plants will also have more room for growth and require watering less frequently. Large containers are usually heavy, so try placing them on dollies with casters to make them easy to move.

Whatever containers you choose, good drainage is necessary to avoid soggy roots, which can lead to root rot. Ideally, you'll want to select containers that have adequate drainage holes. For outdoor pots, you won't need to purchase drainage saucers; water that becomes stagnant in these can become a breeding ground for damaging pests. And don't despair if you find just the right pot only to discover that it has no drain holes! There is a way to remedy the problem of favorite pots with poor drainage (see "Pot Luck" on page 114).

CHOOSING DECORATIVE PLANTS

As you shop for plants, keep your choices simple. You can always add complexity to your garden once you've established a basic plan. Start out by determining the visual effect you hope to achieve—formal or informal, permanent or seasonal, or a combined effect. Choose colors that lift your spirit and scents that take your breath away. Bright aromatic displays will soon invite butterflies, bees, and hummingbirds.

On the practical side, consider the amount of available sunlight, as well as the rate of growth and scale of plants that will thrive in your space. You don't want "creepers and climbers" showing up as unwelcome guests in your neighbor's backyard!

While a few plants prefer solid ground to container life (roses and deciduous clematis fall into this cate-gory), almost any plant will thrive in a suitable container if it's given proper light, water, nutrients, and periodic grooming. For visual variety, mix annuals with perennials or combine common plants with more exotic ones.

EDIBLE PLANTS

For people whose yards aren't large enough for an orchard or garden, containers provide a wonderful way to grow fruits and vegetables. Fresh green lettuce, sweet young carrots, radishes, tomatoes, peppers, and strawberries all grow well in pots, and with a few extra-large containers, you can even establish your own orchard by planting dwarf fruit trees. If you'd like to try your hand at growing edibles this way, it helps to keep a few tips in mind.

Never use a container that has at some point held a substance toxic to humans or plants. If you use wooden containers, make sure the wood hasn't been treated with a preservative. (Naturally rot-resistant woods such as cedar or redwood are fine.) Make sure your pots are large enough to support the plants once they're mature, and use only containers with drainage holes in them.

When growing edibles, avoid the light, soil-free potting mixtures that are sold for houseplants. They lack the organic matter required to keep edible plants healthy.

Instead, select a potting soil that's rich in organic nutrients. Commercial potting soils generally provide enough fertilizer for about eight weeks' growth, but vegetables and fruits will require periodic use of a water-soluble fertilizer after that.

No container garden is really complete without a collection of aromatic herbs: basil, oregano, parsley, chives,

rosemary, and thyme. Whether they're planted in separate pots or together in a large container, herbs provide decorative appeal and culinary pleasures.

CREATING YOUR DESIGN

To achieve a balanced design, select plants that suit their containers' forms and the materials from which they're made. In ornamental pots or works of art, use upright plants that comple-ment rather than overwhelm the container. Less attractive containers can be dressed with flowers cascading over their rims. Plant colorful containers with flowers of matching or contrasting hues. For optimal effect, group pots in key locations—beside a garden gate, along a stairway (shown lower right) or at the edge of a pond. To give structure to your design, use pedestals, posts, and stands that will vary the

heights of plants. For a less structured look, scatter pots throughout surrounding beds and terraces, or along a favorite path. And when you tire of a design, just rearrange the landscape by mixing and matching containers and plants to create a new one.

"POT LUCK": RECIPES FOR SUCCESSFUL CONTAINER GARDENING

The tools for container gardening are few and simple. You'll need a small hand trowel, preferably forged steel with a wooden handle; a pair of good-quality pruning shears; and a watering can or hose with an adjustable outlet. Before setting plants in any used container, clean the container thoroughly with dish soap and hot water. Then sterilize the container by scrubbing it with a ten-percent bleach solution or with a handful of rock salt in a mixture of two parts white vinegar and one part water. Rinse thoroughly when you're finished; Even organic cleaning agents can harm plants. Small pots can be run through the dishwasher.

When you're ready to begin the planting process, first place a layer of drainage materials in the bottom of your container: marble chips, pebbles, pottery shards, or polystyrene "peanuts" will all work well. Spread a one-inch-deep layer in each small pot and a two-inch-deep layer in each larger one. The type of potting soil

flat rose at its end. Apply the water directly to the soil, not to the foliage.

Check the moisture levels of containers daily at the edges and near the center, and water early in the day when the air is cool. During the growing season, fertilize the plants once every seven to ten days. Feed them in the morning, after watering, using water-soluble plant food or organic fertilizers (fish emulsion, liquid kelp, or blood meal).

As part of your ongoing plant-care program, remove faded flowers daily to encourage new growth and prevent certain plants from going to seed. To deadhead properly, cut or pinch below the flower pod, just above the node, rather than pulling the flower from its pod. Using sharp, clean pruning shears, remove all diseased, dead, or weak growth to promote health and preserve the shape of your plants. Try to prune sensitively, cutting at an angle, away from the leaf joint.

you use will also influence drainage, so be sure to buy one that contains perlite or coarse sand. (To remedy poor drainage in pots you've already planted, carefully remove the plant and soil. Then use an electric drill—and a masonry bit if the container is made of cement, clay, or stone—to bore extra holes in the container's bottom.)

Fill the container with potting soil to within two inches of its rim. Gently remove the plant from its cell pack or pot and spread its roots. Use your trowel to dig a hole in the potting soil. Then insert the plant, add potting soil, and press it down firmly. Water the plant well using either a watering can or a long-handled hose wand with a

REPELLING PLANT PESTS

When pests become a problem, avoid using chemical pesticides if possible. Many pests can be kept at bay by placing unpeeled garlic cloves one inch deep in the soil, near the rim of each pot—about three cloves for a 14-inch pot. To deter "crawlers," sprinkle cayenne pepper on the soil near the rim of the pot. Keep slugs away from tender foliage by placing a shallow container (a jar lid or tin tray) of beer near the bases of the pots. As an alternative to chemical sprays, try making your own organic spray. Simply add the tobacco from four cigarettes, four crushed garlic cloves, one teaspoon of white pepper, two tablespoons of liquid insecticidal soap, and two tablespoons of ammonia to two quarts of hot water. Steep the mixture for several hours and then strain it thoroughly. Spray plants three times a week until health is restored.

Moss-Lined Hanging Basket

A cheerful profusion of color contained in a moss-lined basket will be a stunning eye-catcher, enlivening your garden with variety and visual interest. Its earthy texture, with plants trailing in the breeze, lures us back to nature and is perfect for any setting. As well as their aesthetic charm, hanging baskets offer a practical and attractive way to bring visual balance or contrast to your surroundings.

MATERIALS & TOOLS

- Open-mesh wire basket or other open-weave container
- Green sheet moss (available at garden centers, craft stores, and florists)
- Plastic sheeting
- Top-grade potting soil
- Plants
- Trowel
- Scissors
- Wire hanger or wall mount
- Slow-release plant food

TIPS

- Be sure to match your plant selection with the hanging site to ensure proper growing conditions.
- Over-watering your basket can be a problem. To check for moisture, gently insert your finger into the soil. Water only when the soil feels dry.
- Replenish plants in your hanging basket by replacing them with others. When bulbs have stopped blooming, for example, replace them with spring or summer annuals. (Grocery stores and garden centers are excellent sources for blooming annuals and bulbs.)

Instructions

1 Water the plants in their packaged containers so they'll be well hydrated when you place them in the soil. To hydrate the sheet moss and make it easier to use, allow it to soak in water for 10 to 15 minutes. Then squeeze it out to eliminate excess moisture.

2 Line the basket with a layer of damp moss, placing the more attractive green side out. Adjust the thickness of the layer to eliminate any holes. To check for shallow spots, hold the pot up to the light; then add more moss if necessary.

3 Cut a layer of plastic sheeting to fit the size of the basket. Using the scissors, punch drainage holes, spacing them about 1" apart. Then place the plastic on top of the moss to form an inner lining that will conserve moisture.

4 Fill the basket half full with potting soil. For proper drainage, use a quality, name-brand soil with a combination of peat, perlite, and bark.

5 Position the basket on an upturned bucket or pot to allow sufficient clearance for trailing or cascading plants. Plant trailing plants such as English ivy first. Insert small clumps or segments from cell packs around the perimeter of the potting soil. Cover the roots with soil, and press the soil gently with your fingers or trowel to eliminate air pockets. Then give the basket a gentle shake to settle the contents.

6 Plant the largest plant next, either in the center of the basket (if you plan to hang the basket) or toward the back (if you plan to display the basket against a wall).

7 Fill in with remaining plants— tallest to shortest, in descending order—working either from the back or center to the outside edge of the basket. Remember to firm the plants, add more soil as needed, and periodically shake everything down. If you plan to hang the basket rather than display it with a wall bracket, be sure to leave room for the hanging chains.

8 When all the plants have been placed, add additional potting soil if necessary to cover the roots completely and fill in any gaps between plants. Then cover the soil with a thin layer of sheet moss.

9 Water the basket gently but thoroughly with a diluted solution of slow-release fertilizer, until you see water trickling out around the base. Allow the basket to drain completely before you hang it.

10 Attach the wire hanger to the basket, being careful not to damage surrounding plants. If you prefer a wall display, secure the basket with a wall mount or a heavy-duty nail.

11 Mist the plants for the first week or two, until they're established in their new home.

VARIATION

For a variation on your planting theme, either select a different basket material, as shown above, or create a lush, rounded look by arranging some of your trailing plants to extend through the sides of the wire basket.

Start by placing a thin layer of damp moss in the bottom of the basket. Fit a layer of plastic sheeting over it, punching drainage holes as described in step 3. Arrange a shallow layer of potting soil on top of the plastic liner and insert your small trailing plants through the lowest openings in the basket. Cover their roots with soil and press gently to eliminate air pockets. Continue this process, until you reach the top of the basket. Line the basket with moss as you progress upward, followed by additional layers of soil and plants. Avoid adding too many plants; three layers is usually adequate to create the desired look.

Garden Tools and Storage

What do gardening "experts" use to dig, cut, rake, and shape their prized outdoor spaces? Designer gadgets tempt professionals and weekend gardeners alike, but, in truth, the most useful tools are the same reliable ones that have been cultivating for centuries. Basic is best: sturdy spades and metal rakes, humble trowels and hoes, and perhaps a long-handled garden fork. Whether passed down from your grandparents or ordered from a glossy mail-order catalog, tools should be exceptionally well made, lovingly maintained, and carefully stored when they're not in use.

TOOL SELECTION TIPS

■ Buy your tools one at a time, and buy the highest-quality tools you can afford. If your budget is tight, by all means search yard sales and flea markets—just don't compromise quality. Inexpensive, secondhand garden gear is hardly a bargain if it's flawed.

■ Find tools made with forged or tempered high-carbon or stainless steel blades and with handles made from straight-grained ash or hickory (or high-strength fiberglass).

■ Look for a strong blade extension that surrounds the handle completely, and avoid tools with painted wooden handles—the color may deceptively camouflage knots or flaws in the wood.

■ Use tools that "fit"—that are the right size and weight for you. A good tool should feel like an extension of your own hands rather than an awkward burden; it should make your job easier and not more difficult. A shiny new spade that's too heavy to lift or a trowel that's too large to grip will doubtless spend its working life in your garden shed.

DIGGING AND CULTIVATING TOOLS

The trusty hand trowel, with its scoop-shaped pointed blade, is the garden tool that you'll probably use most often. Look for a trowel with a forged, heavy-gauge metal blade and an easy-grip handle. A three- or four-clawed hand rake makes soil cultivation and hand weeding a cinch.

A garden spade with a rounded blade is indispensable. You'll use it to cultivate garden beds and dig holes for

sweeping cousin, the heavy-gauge metal garden rake is ideal for combing through and leveling the soil in garden beds. To turn the compost pile, aerate soil, or divide perennials, use a pitchfork with thin, strong tines.

CUTTING TOOLS

In addition to digging, scraping, and turning, you'll also be doing some clipping and chopping in your backyard. For these tasks, you'll need gardening scissors, grass shears, pruning shears, and an asparagus fork. A sturdy pair of gardening scissors, with reinforced handles, is the perfect tool for cutting flowers and may also be used for light topiary work. Grass shears come in handy for trimming the growth that borders your garden walkway. The best grass shears have long, sharp, scissorlike blades; reinforcing springs; and metal squeeze handles. Pruning shears can manage thicker stems up to ¾ inch in diameter. Finally, an asparagus fork is the tool you'll turn to when battling excessive root growth; its 12- to 18-inch metal shank has a sharp, V-notched head at the tip that will trim the roots of plants you love and sever the long taproots of those you don't.

large plants. Shovels with rectangular blades are best for moving gravel and large quantities of soil. Remember as you shop for a shovel that although larger, heavier models penetrate more deeply and hold more soil, unless you have the strength to wield them, they'll wear you out in a matter of minutes. Don't be embarrassed to "try on" a new spade just as you would a new pair of shoes—go on, charade a bed excavation right there in the aisle of the hardware store. The salespeople may giggle, but you won't make the mistake of buying yourself a strained muscle or a slipped disk.

No weekend gardener should be without a metal garden rake. Unlike the long, flexible tines of its leaf-

TOOL MAINTENANCE

Every minute that you spend protecting your tools from moisture, cleaning and sharpening their blades, and caring for their wooden handles will better their performance and lengthen their working lives. Tool maintenance is easier than it sounds. Just set aside five minutes at the end of each gardening day to perform a few simple tasks. Rust is the greatest foe to garden gear; metal heads and shanks that take regular nose dives into moist soil will inevitably face the risk of rust. Regularly cleaning and oiling blades is the best way to battle this problem. (Though rustproof fiberglass tools have recently become available, steel garden tools remain the most popular.)

If tool blades are coated with compacted soil, hose them down and dry

them thoroughly, then wipe them with an oily rag to prevent rust. A cleaner, more convenient option may be to set up a tool maintenance station: Fill a container with a mixture of sand and motor oil and plunge freshly-rinsed blades into the sand a few times. The coarse mixture will scour any remnants of soil from the blade and will protect the metal by leaving an oily residue. If at any point you do notice light rust setting into a metal tool, the best remedy is steel wool and good old-fashioned elbow grease. For heavier rust, use an electric drill with a rotating wire-brush attachment.

Now, check the wooden handles and sand away any splinters that may have formed during the day. Once or twice a year, rub the handles down with linseed oil to preserve the wood, or paint them with exterior-grade paint. (A brightly colored handle has the added advantage of being easy to spot when you've accidentally misplaced a tool in the yard.)

Finally, keep all tool blades sharp; dull blades will double your labor. You may sharpen the blades yourself with a whetstone or electric rotating sharpener, or take them to a professional sharpening service.

TOOL STORAGE

If you're the kind of gardener who thinks of "tool storage" as propping your rakes and shovels against the exterior wall of your garage and toss-ing the trowel into an empty basket under its eaves, you might want to read this section carefully. Here, observe how a few simple habits will help you preserve the tools you own, prevent serious accidents, and save you hours of frantic searching for lost tools.

Organizing your tools isn't critical, but it will help you keep your sanity during your plight for a better backyard (nothing is as comforting as the sight of your tools lined up on a pristine wall-length tool rack!). Also, when storage space is limited, a system of organization will help you make wise use of available space. Traditional racks and cupboards come in an array of shapes, sizes, and materials and are

page 122 for instructions).

If you're gardening on a budget, you may be hard-pressed to invest in a fancy tool rack or shed. If that's the case—or if you just want to add a playful touch to your garden—then get creative! Imagine how you might transform found objects into functional storage gear. Fasten the head of an old metal rake to a shed wall, with the metal tines pointing outward. Then use the tines as hooks for hanging smaller tools and gloves, or hang tools by their heads (shown on page 119). Salvage the frame of an old umbrella, hang it upside down, and drape your oily tool-wiping rags and lengths of wound rope over the metal tips. Or suspend a bicycle wheel horizontally, hang S-hooks from the spokes, and use these hooks to hold your lightweight hand tools. Begin to consider the possibilities for creative storage . . . and realize that they are nearly endless.

No matter what kind of storage system you develop, put away all garden tools as soon as you've finished using them. It's maddening to waste an hour of a sunny Saturday tracking tools down, and it's dangerous to find one by stepping on its grass-disguised tines as you amble across your lawn! Additionally, make sure that your tools—and all garden chemicals—stay well out of reach of children and pets. The ideal tool-storage site will have a door with a lock.

widely available at home-improvement and garden centers. Pegboard is indispensable for organizing tools. Arrange your tools on a pegboard, using a marker to outline the shape of each. That way, you'll know just where to place your pitchfork the next time you put it away, and if it's ever missing you'll notice right away.

See if this scenario sounds familiar: You're on your hands and knees weeding with slavish devotion when a neighbor waves hello from next door. You set down the hand rake just for a minute to say hi—then wind up gabbing for an hour and forget where you left off. Because tools are most often misplaced while we're working, it's wise to invest in some sort of carry-all to keep you organized on the job. Portable storage options might include a woven basket, a wooden tote, or a canvas tool belt (see

Gardener's Tool Belt

This method of toting tools has been used by carpenters over the ages. You'll never lose track of your spade again with a big, roomy pocket to stow it in. And plenty more space remains for seed packets, gloves, and other garden gear. Judging by its handsome look and unique design, you'd think this undertaking is for experienced sewers only. If you're a beginner, you may indeed want to practice on scrap fabric first, but you'll be surprised at the ease of the project!

MATERIALS & TOOLS

- Heavy-duty sewing scissors
- Heavy denim, 1 yard
- Lightweight cotton (in a print or color that complements the denim), 1 yard
- Straight pins
- Tape measure
- Woven trim/seam binding, 7 yards
- Sewing machine
- Iron
- Belt strapping, 2" wide, 5 feet in length
- Belt clasp, 2" wide
- 2 slides, 2" wide (to secure excess strapping)

TIPS

- Unless you choose a fabric lighter than the denim used here, you'll need to equip your sewing machine with an extra-heavy needle and thread before beginning this project.
- Working with trim can be tricky because of its narrow width. When sewing, always take care to catch the back side of the trim in your stitch line. Also, it may be easier to work with the trim in one long piece, cutting it as you stitch, rather than using exact lengths from the onset.
- You'll find belt strapping and clasps at camping-supply or outdoor specialty stores.

CUTTING LIST

QUANTITY	DESCRIPTION	DIMENSION
4	Side-pocket backs	4½" x 15"
4	Side-pocket fronts	9" x 9"
1	Center-pocket back	9" x 15"
1	Tall Center-pocket front	9" x 9"
1	Short Center-pocket front	9" x 6"

Instructions

1 Use the sewing scissors to cut each of the items on the cutting list from both the denim and the cotton cloth.

2 Align each of the denim pieces to its corresponding cotton-lining piece, wrong sides together, and pin them together. For each side-pocket piece, the top will be one 4½" edge; for each center-pocket piece, the top will be one 9" edge.

3 Machine-baste the lining to the denim along the sides and bottoms for all six pocket fronts so that your stitches are ¼" from the raw edges. Turn all the pocket fronts so the denim and cotton are right side out.

4 Position the trim along one edge of a pocket front so that it encases the raw edges of the fabric (this will be the top of the pocket). Stitch the trim in place ¼" from the edge. Repeat this process for the five remaining pocket fronts.

5 Make a ½" fold (wrong sides together) along the top edge of one cotton back piece and another along the top edge of its corresponding denim back piece. Press the folds into place with the iron. Machine-baste along the raw edges of the remaining the sides and bottom, ¼" in from the raw edges. Turn so the denim and cotton are right side out. Repeat this entire step for all remaining back pieces.

6 To create the center front pocket, layer the pieces together as follows, denim sides up: center-pocket back, then tall center-pocket front, then short center-pocket front. Align the pieces along their bottom and side edges. Machine-baste the assembly ¼" from the aligned edges. Position trim along the full length of the bottom and sides and stitch into place.

7 To create the side pockets, layer the side pocket front on top of the side-pocket back, denim sides up. Align the side and bottom edges, and pin the denim and lining together.

Then, take up the excess fabric of the pocket front and form two equal-sized pleats in the pocket front fabric. Pin the pleats into place, and press them flat with the iron. Machine-baste along the sides and bottom, leaving a ¼" edge. Position trim along the full length of the sides and back, and stitch into place.

8 For the belt casing, create a 2¾" fold over the top edges to the back sides of each of the five pocket backs. Press the fold into place with the iron. Stitch very close to the fold, stopping at the trim. Stitch again 2¼" below that seam, again stopping at the trim and being sure to catch the back edge of the fold in the stitch line.

9 Insert the strapping through each of the casings, and attach the buckle and slides. Adjust the length to fit, load up with tools, and head out for a day of gardening!

GARDEN ART AND WHIMSY

earth

Upper Left: This mushroom-shaped, poured concrete planter doubles as a rustic garden table. While it might not accommodate an elegant—or practical—dinner setting, it does serve up fragrant herbs in a unique and appealing style!

Upper Right: The hard, industrial appeal of Christopher Mello's scrap-metal garden in Asheville, NC, is softened by a dancing, organic line of tiny hens and chicks *(Sempervivum)*. Be daring with your container gardening—realizing, of course, that not every potted experiment will yield flourishing foliage!

Bottom: The ancient serenity of a Japanese rock garden provides a rare and wonderful treat, especially when perched high atop the Appalachian mountains like this one. While your kids might rather you convert such a vast space into a playing field, do sanction some area of the yard for your own peaceful reflection.

Left: A well-built retaining wall will add true panache to your terraced garden. Go a step further, though, and cover yours in bright mosaic! This one, created by ceramicist Carlos Alves and students at Penland School of Craft, features handmade tiles abstractly assembled to depict a nearby river and forest.

Above: A suburban backyard teeming with wildlife? Well, sort of: These lovely creatures are less wont to frolic than real forest friends, and their fur is a bit more prickly to the touch. Still, they add an undeniable charm to the garden. Grown on shaped wire treillage, these living sculptures are proof that a pair of shears and a sense of humor can work wonders for your backyard.

Left: Though your budget may prevent you from splurging on fancy outdoor ornaments, you'll still have plenty of trinkets with which to decorate your garden. Using simple, natural objects such as twigs, moss, or the stones shown here, you can create playfully primitive shrines and other areas of interest in the garden.

Acknowledgments

PHOTOGRAPHY

Three very accommodating, very spirited North Carolina photographers are chiefly responsible for the images in this book:

Evan Bracken
Light Reflections, Hendersonville

pages 5 (top), 17 (bottom), 23–25, 34, 36, 37 (upper left), 41 (right) 51, 53 (left), 59 (bottom), 70, 76–80, 82 (left), 84, 86 (right), 89 (top), 92, 94, 108, 109, 112, 114, 115 (bottom), 116–119, 124 (top).

Robin Dreyer
Burnsville

pages 9 (top, middle), 22, 16, 10, 23 (bottom), 33 (bottom), 35 (top left, middle left), 39, 40, 41 (bottom left), 50, 57 (top right), 59 (middle), 62, 64–65, 87 (right), 88, 89 (middle, bottom), 90, 95 (bottom), 96, 97, 99, 104, 106, 107, 124 (bottom), 125 (top left).

Richard Hasselberg
Black Mountain

pages 8,12,14, 15, 17 (top), 22(bottom left), 28, 29, 38, 41 (top left), 45–47, 56 (left), 60 (right), 66, 92 (top), 93 (bottom), 95 (top), 110, 112, 122, 123.

Supplementary photography courtesy of:
T.A. Allan, Out 'n' About Treehouse Resort, Cave Junction, OR (treehouses.com), page 75; Richard Reames, Arborsmith Studios (Williams, OR), pages 5 (bottom), 59 (top), 87 (left); Ariane Bicho (San Francisco), page 86 (left); Crate and Barrel, pages 3, 19, 98; Gardener's Supply Co., Burlington, VT (1-800-863-1700, gardeners.com), pages 33 (middle), 44 (left), 52, 56 (right), 58, 82 (right), 105; Garden Image® (gardenimage.com), pages 6, 18, 26, 27, 30 (above left, bottom), 43, 100, 101 (above left), 102, 125; ©Robert Gusick, page 74; ©Good Directions, Inc., Danbury, CT (windstock.com), page 60 (left); Monrovia (Azusa, CA), pages 33 (top right), 35 (bottom left, top right, and bottom right); Hatteras Hammocks® (Greenville, NC), page 73; ©Jerry Pavia, pages 4 (bottom), 69, 31, 125 (top right); ©Leonard Phillips, page 57 (bottom); Plow and Hearth, Inc., pages 11, 44 (right), 48, 49, 53 (right), 68, 72; Smith and Hawken, pages 4 (top), 32, 42, 54, 57 (left), 61, 91, 115 (bottom), 120, 121; ©George Ramig (Asheville, NC) page 30 (top right).

PROPS

Many thanks to the following retail outfitters for the loan and/or donation of props: Cherry Blossom Gardens, Prarie, MN (www.japanesegifts.com), Early Music Shop, (Asheville, NC), B.B. Barns, (Asheville, NC), Grovewood Gallery, (www.grovewood.com), Gardener's Cottage (Asheville, NC), and Pier One Imports.

LOCATIONS

A number of North Carolina residents and business owners have been gracious enough to allow us to photograph the grounds of their stunning properties. All have demonstrated patience and generosity that have eased the task at hand:

Oscar and Sarah Bailey, Burnsville
Wally, Conor, and Star Bowen, Asheville
Marilyn and Jerry Cade, Burnsville
Diane Rodgers Claybrook, Asheville
John Cram, Asheville
Ian and Jo Lydia Craven, Burnsville
Eve Davis, Hank and Ivy Bed and
    Breakfast, Barnardsville
Donna Jean Dreyer, Burnsville
Mignon Durham, Penland
Susan Fennelly and Ken Minnich,
    Asheville
Robert and Jacqueline Glasgow, Beaufort
    House Bed and Breakfast, Asheville
Vanessa Osborne, Grove Park Inn/
Grovewood Gallery, Asheville
Penland School of Crafts, Penland
Peggy Farrell Tibbits, Burnsville
Gary and Patricia Wiles, Cumberland
    Falls Bed and Breakfast, Asheville
Carol Ann Winter, A Hill House Bed
    and Breakfast, Asheville
Wayne Yordy, The Lion and the Rose
    Bed and Breakfast, Asheville

PROJECT DESIGN

For their ingenuity and flexibility, we are grateful to the following project designers: Joe Archibald, kneeling pad, page 110; Kevin Barnes, birdbath trellis, page 84; Larry Burda, wind vane, page 62; Eve Davis, hanging basket, page 116; Terry Taylor, wind chime, page 66; Kim Tibbals-Thompson, tool belt, page 122; Tzadi Turrou, mosaic stones, page 96.

EDITORIAL CONTRIBUTION

Thanks to Malaprop's Bookstore (Asheville, NC) for allowing us to roam and pillage their stacks for research purposes. Much appreciation goes to Julie Abbott and Carolyn Bertram for their supplementary writing, research, and proofreading. Without the indexing abilities and cheerleading of Catharine Sutherland; the encouragement of Chris Rich; the design prowess and brotherly heckling of Thom Gaines; or the mentorship of Kathy Sheldon, this book would not have been possible. Thanks to Clyde Cook, Jr. for planting the seed.

Metric Conversions

Length

Inches	CM		
1/8	0.3	19	48.3
1/4	0.6	20	50.8
3/8	1.0	21	53.3
1/2	1.3	22	55.9
5/8	1.6	23	58.4
3/4	1.9	24	61.0
7/8	2.2	25	63.5
1	2.5	26	66.0
1 1/4	3.2	27	68.6
1 1/2	3.8	28	71.1
1 3/4	4.4	29	73.7
2	5.1	30	76.2
2 1/2	6.4	31	78.7
3	7.6	32	81.3
3 1/2	8.9	33	83.8
4	10.2	34	86.4
4 1/2	11.4	35	88.9
5	12.7	36	91.4
6	15.2	37	94.0
7	17.8	38	96.5
8	20.3	39	99.1
9	22.9	40	101.6
10	25.4	41	104.1
11	27.9	42	106.7
12	30.5	43	109.2
13	33.0	44	111.8
14	35.6	45	114.3
15	38.1	46	116.8
16	40.6	47	119.4
17	43.2	48	121.9
18	45.7	49	124.5
		50	127.0

Volume

1 fluid ounce = 29.6 ml
1 pint = 473 ml
1 quart = 946 ml
1 gallon (128 fl. oz.) = 3.785 liters

liters x .2642 = gallons
liters x 2.11 = pints
liters x 33.8 = fluid ounces
gallons x 3.785 = liters
gallons x .1337 = cubic feet
cubic feet x 7.481 = gallons
cubic feet x 28.32 = liters

Weight

0.035 ounces = 1 gram
1 ounce = 28.35 grams
1 pound = 453.6 grams

grams x .0353 = ounces
grams x .0022 = pounds
ounces x 28.35 = grams
pounds x 453.6 = grams
tons (short) x 907.2 = kilograms
tons (metric) x 2205 = pounds
kilograms x .0011 = tons (short)
pounds x .00045 = tons (metric)

Bibliography

Allison, James. *Water in the Garden.* Toronto: Little, Brown and Company, Bulfinch Press, 1991.

Anthenat, Kathy S. *American Tree Houses and Play Houses.* Crozet, Va.: Betterway Publications, 1991.

Blomgren, Paige Gilchrist. *Making Paths and Walkways: Creative Ideas and Simple Techniques.* Asheville, N.C.: Lark Books, 1999.

Burda, Cindy. *Wind Toys That Spin, Sing, Whirl and Twirl.* New York: Sterling Publishing Co., 1999.

Coleman, Eliot. *The New Organic Grower's Four-Season Harvest: How to Harvest Fresh Organic Vegetables from Your Home.* Post Mills, Vt.: Chelsea Green Publishing Company, 1992.

Cox, Jeff and Jerry Pavia. *Decorating Your Garden.* New York: Abbeville Press Publishers, 1999.

Erler, Catriona Tudor. *Garden Rooms: Creating and Decorating Outdoor Garden Spaces.* Alexandria, Va.: Time-Life Books, 1999.

Jay, Roni. *Gardens of the Spirit: Create Your Own Sacred Spaces.* New York: Sterling Publishing Co., 1998.

LaLiberte, Katherine and Ben Watson. *Gardener's Supply Company Passport to Gardening: A Sourcebook for the 21st-Century Gardener.* White River Junction, Vt.: Chelsea Green Publishing Company, 1997.

Lombardi, Margherita and Cristiana Serra Zanetti. *Topiaria e Sculture Verdi.* Italy: R.C.S. Libri S.p.A., 1996. Translated by Sterling Publishing Co., under the title *Topiary Basics: The Art of Shaping Plants in Gardens and Containers.* New York: Sterling Publishing Co., 1999.

Taylor, Gordon and Guy Cooper. *Gardens of Obsession.* London: Orion Publishing Group, Weidenfeld and Nicholson, 1999.

Yard and Garden Projects: Easy, Step-by-Step Plans and Designs for Beautiful Outdoor Spaces. Alexandria, Va.: Time-Life Books, 1998.

Index